EXPLORING FUTURE OPTIONS

CRISD

DIRKSEN JR. HIGH SCHOOL
203 South Midland Avenue
Joliet, IL 60436

EXPLORING FUTURE OPTIONS
A Career Development Curriculum for Middle School Students

CRSO

Nancy Perry
Zark VanZandt

international debate education association
New York • Amsterdam • Brussels

Published by

international debate education association

400 West 59th Street / New York, NY 10019

Activity sheets may be downloaded from www.idebate.org/exploringfutureoptions.htm

Library of Congress Cataloging-in-Publication Data

Perry, Nancy, 1934-
  Exploring future options: a career development curriculum for middle-school students / Nancy Perry, Zark VanZandt.
       p. cm.
  ISBN 1-932716-14-9
  ISBN 978-1-932716-14-6

  1. Career education--Curricula. 2. Career education--Study and teaching (Middle school) 3. Vocational guidance. I. Van-Zandt, Zark.
  II. Title.
   LC1037.P42 2005
   370.11'3--dc22

                                                      2005022982

Design by Hernan Bonomo
Printed in the USA

 IDEBATE Press Books

Contents

Unit Three: Career-Planning: How Do I Get There?

Appendix: A Parent's Guide to Career Decision-Making

PART I
Teacher's Guide

⚬⚬⚬

OVERVIEW

Exploring Future Options provides you with a flexible framework for introducing career development to middle-school students. We encourage you add or adapt lesson plans, background information, and activities to meet your needs, and to develop additional ways of working with parents and the community.

Before you begin the curriculum, familiarize yourself with the concepts of career development and their importance to your students. This curriculum provides enough background information for lessons and activities to help you teach these concepts with confidence. Because each lesson builds on the knowledge and/or skills taught in the previous lessons, follow the curriculum sequentially.

HOW TO USE *EXPLORING FUTURE OPTIONS*

Exploring Future Options is divided into two parts: Teacher's Guide and The Curriculum

Part 1: Teacher's Guide is divided into 5 sections:

Overview—introduces the curriculum and lists teaching objectives and/or student outcomes.

Career Development—defines career development and delineates the foundations on which modern practice is built. The section explains the career-building concepts that guide the curriculum and establishes the importance of career development in every student's life.

Effective Teaching Strategies—suggests effective teaching strategies based on middle-school characteristics.

About the Curriculum—gives an overview of the lessons and explains how each is formatted.

Student Portfolio—describes how to construct student portfolios.

Part 2: The Curriculum is divided into three units containing a total of 36 sessions. Each unit helps students answer a question essential to their career development.

Unit One: Self-Knowledge helps students answer the question "Who am I?" Self-knowledge includes interests, abilities, values, and aspirations.

Unit Two: Career Exploration helps students answer the question "Where am I going?" In this section students begin exploring careers and occupations. As they explore, they become aware that the process they use for exploring and making choices is more important than their choice.

Unit Three: Career-Planning helps students answer the question "How do I get there?" The lessons guide them through the decision-making process. Sessions help them develop a long-range perspective so that they can begin making plans about their future education and careers.

As you use this curriculum, remember that you play a vital role in your students' lives now and in the future. You are their guide on the wondrous journey to adulthood. Enjoy the journey!

STUDENT OBJECTIVES

Upon completing this curriculum, students will:

1. Understand the concept of career development.

2. Realize the importance of planning for the future.

3. Understand that they have choices in planning their careers (life work).

4. Grasp the importance of education.

5. See how their current behaviors and attitudes may affect their future.

6. Acquire self-knowledge.

7. Begin exploring the world of work.

8. Realize that planning and preparation for the future begin now.

9. Understand that the process is more important than the choice.

10. Know that career development is a lifelong process.

CAREER DEVELOPMENT

WHAT IS CAREER DEVELOPMENT?

Career development is a process that allows us to gather information about ourselves and apply it to the world of work. It began when we were children, dreaming about what we wanted to be when we grew up. We understood not only that we would have a career but that we could choose what that career would be. However, we did not make these choices in a vacuum. Family, community, school, and national events all influenced our decision. Today, the rapidly shifting global economy demands new ways of looking at our lives. Therefore, the career development process must continue throughout our lifetime.

We have designed *Exploring Future Options* to help middle-school students through the early stages of the career development process. The program takes the students step by step through activities that will help them make informed decisions about possible career choices and the education they will need to pursue them.

Just as the world is changing, so have the definitions we associate with career development. In this curriculum, the following definitions apply:

- **Job:** a position with specific duties and responsibilities; one's source of livelihood.

    Example: I have a job writing programs for Micrographic Industries.

- **Occupation**: a field of study or a similar group of jobs.

    Example: My occupation is astrophysicist.

- **Career**: the sequence of occupations and other life roles that combine to express our commitment to work in our total pattern of self-development.

    Example: I am a parent and spouse who has chosen to be a dancer.

- **Career-building**: the management of the events and roles that shape our life/career.

    Example: I took the appropriate courses and passed the necessary exams to become a dentist. I have been offered an opportunity to teach dentistry. Therefore, I am considering a career change.

THEORIES OF CAREER DEVELOPMENT AND DECISION-MAKING

There are basically two schools of career development theory: structural and developmental.

Structural Theory

The structural school focuses on matching individuals to occupations that mesh with their interests and aptitudes. One example of this type of theory is the **Trait and Factor Theory**.

Developed by Frank Parsons at the beginning of the 20th century, it involves a three-step process in which individuals:

1. Analyze their aptitudes, skills, interests, resources, and other qualities.

2. Investigate the requirements, opportunities, and prospects in different occupations.

3. Use reasoning to connect the information gathered in steps 1 and 2.

Another example of the structural theory is the Theory of Vocational Personalities and Environments, which John Holland developed in the late 20th century. Holland maintained that people in similar occupations had similar personalities and so classified vocational personalities and work environments into six categories as follows:

Realistic (R)

Investigative (I)

Artistic (A)

Social (S)

Enterprising (E)

Conventional (C)

Holland assumed that most people would be a combination of three related personality types. For example, a farmer may be realistic (R), conventional (C), and investigative (I). Therefore, his Holland Code would be RCI.

HOLLAND'S SIX PERSONALITY TYPES

Type	Characteristics	Examples
Realistic (R)	Prefers working with things, tools, and/or animals.	Farmers, skilled trade workers, and engineers
Investigative (I)	Prefers using intelligence and abstract reasoning in disciplined inquiry, data-gathering, and analysis.	Scientists, highly specialized technicians, and mathematicians
Artistic (A)	Highly creative people who concentrate on originality, self-expression, and intuition. They may work with tools to create original works or they may work with people through their expressive media.	Writers, artisans, and performers
Social (S)	Prefers working with people rather than working with things or data.	Counselors, social workers, teachers, and hospitality workers
Enterprising (E)	Seeks and enjoys leadership and persuasion of others for purposes of accomplishing organizational, political, or financial goals.	Salespeople, supervisors, and politicians
Conventional (C)	Enjoys working with data more than people or things.	Accountants, financial workers, and clerical workers

Developmental Theories

These theories are based on the premise that the developmental stages we go through in life influence our choice of work. For example, Donald Super's **Developmental Self-Concept Theory** focuses on career as a lifelong process. He postulates that people change with time and experience and seek careers in which they can express themselves and develop their vocational self-concepts. These self-concepts develop through five stages as follows:

SUPER'S FIVE DEVELOPMENTAL STAGES

Stage	Age	Characteristics
Growth	(–14)	Thinks about interests and abilities; develops general understanding of the work world.
Exploration	(15–24)	Narrows down career choices; ultimately finds a job or gets final training.
Establishment	(25–44)	Becomes committed to an occupation; moves up in the field.
Maintenance	(45–64)	Continues adjustment to improve position; might shift attention to family.
Decline	(65–)	Plans for retirement; retires.

Super based his theory on a series of propositions that emphasize career maturity, self-concept, and multiple life roles. His propositions state that:

- People differ in their abilities and personalities, needs, values, interests, traits, and sell-concepts.

- People are qualified by virtue of their characteristics for a number of occupations.

- Each occupation requires a characteristic pattern of abilities and personality traits with tolerances wide enough to allow a variety of individuals within the occupation.

- People change with time and experience in a series of life stages.

- The process of career development is essentially that of developing and implementing occupational self-concepts that are based on career maturity, i.e., the readiness of the individual to cope with the demands of the work.

John Krumboltz's **Social Learning Theory** stresses the importance of environmental conditions and learning experiences in career choice. He theorizes that people choose their careers based on what they have learned. Krumboltz emphasizes three main forms of learning experiences:

- Reinforcement: People learn from the reinforcement they receive from certain behaviors. These can be both positive (praise, money) and negative (threats, punishment).

- Modeling: People learn by directly or indirectly observing others (TV, reading).

- Classical conditioning: People learn by associating events with previous experiences.

Krumboltz believes that decision-making is a learned process that we must learn for use in all areas of life, including career development. Because he emphasizes learning and experience, he recommends coordinated career guidance programs to help individuals explore their options. And, since modeling is a powerful form of learning, he stresses that career counselors need to provide students with opportunities to observe people working in a wide variety of fields.

Exploring Future Options draws from both schools. This curriculum offers students activities that encourage them to identify and classify their knowledge of themselves and explore the various occupations that might match their characteristics. It stresses that career development is a lifelong process. There is not just one "perfect job" for each person because we and our world change. Our program emphasizes the value of decision-making as a life skill and encourages modeling and mentoring as important learning strategies.

GUIDING PRINCIPLES OF CAREER-BUILDING

Five career-building principles are especially effective in working with young people. All are based on a central premise: Instead of focusing on the big decision, young people must look at the big picture of their life. These five principles are:

1. **Change Is Constant.** Our world is changing at an unprecedented rate; many of the jobs of the 21st century have yet to be invented. Therefore, we need a fluid approach to career-planning. We must recognize that career decision-making is a continuous process, not a one-time event.

   We must also learn that our decisions will change with our circumstances. We make the decisions that seem best given our interests, needs, and opportunities at a particular time. These may, and probably will, change. We may have to forego some opportunities but, in return, we gain other experiences. No choice is perfect; all have their pluses and minuses.

2. **Learning Is Ongoing.** When we recognize that the world is constantly changing, it becomes apparent that learning and career-building must be continuous processes. Because learning is so important, we must learn not only specific skills and content, but we must also "learn to learn." Lifelong learning takes place informally, by experiencing and doing, as well as formally, in classroom settings.

3. **Follow Your Heart.** We must learn where our "heart" lies. Fear of failure often discourages us from exploring our dreams. We need to learn to trust ourselves. Flexibility and adaptability are essential in our rapidly changing world. We need to encourage our children to take calculated risks and learn from their failures.

4. **Focus on the Journey.** We must learn to gain meaning from our personal journey through life rather than from achieving a goal. In a changing world, doggedly pursuing a specific goal may become futile. The goal can disappear before we reach it.

   We must establish broad visions of the future that set a general direction, but not a specific target. Our life situations should dictate where we focus our greatest energy. Sometimes we have to deal with immediate concerns; other times we can focus on our enduring needs. But for ongoing life/career satisfaction, we must strive to satisfy both.

5. **Access Your Allies.** We often value our independence, but in reality "we can't do it alone." We need the help and support of people we trust in each aspect of our life/career. These people, whether they be family members, friends, co-workers, fellow students, or bosses, have our best interests at heart. They can help us make decisions and network with others who may be helpful to us.

```
┌─────────────────────────────────────────────────────────┐
│  FIVE GUIDING PRINCIPLES OF CAREER-BUILDING             │
│                                                          │
│   • CHANGE IS CONSTANT                                   │
│                                                          │
│   • LEARNING IS ONGOING                                  │
│                                                          │
│   • FOLLOW YOUR HEART                                    │
│                                                          │
│   • FOCUS ON THE JOURNEY                                 │
│                                                          │
│   • ACCESS YOUR ALLIES                                   │
│                                                          │
└─────────────────────────────────────────────────────────┘
```

WHY CAREER DEVELOPMENT IS IMPORTANT TO STUDENTS

The Changing Workplace

There is no doubt that the workplace has changed. Technology has generated a new type of workplace. The importance of the service sector is increasing while the manufacturing sector is declining. Machines can now do repetitive tasks, while improved transportation and technology have reduced worldwide communication to seconds. With the emphasis on service and the ability of companies to produce goods anywhere, competition, both among businesses and workers is now global.

The Changing Workforce

The new workplace has generated a new workforce. In the global economy, our children will be competing for jobs with the Chinese, Indians, and Irish. In order to compete globally, companies are cutting costs by sending jobs overseas. They are also abandoning traditional employer–employee relationships and turning to outsourcing. Many now use independent contractors who work on a fee-for-service basis rather than in-house workers who require not only a salary but also expensive benefits. Companies are hiring individuals to work part time rather than a full workweek. Some people share jobs, and others telecommute. In the new workplace, workers are selling a service—their knowledge and skills. Even those in traditional employer–employee relationships are finding changed expectations in the workplace. The 21st. century workplace requires that all workers be

- adaptable
- capable of communicating
- entrepreneurial
- responsible for their own actions
- self-motivated
- service oriented
- skilled and knowledgeable

Will our children be ready for this new workplace? Are they willing and able to take the responsibility for managing their own lives? Are they entrepreneurial? Are they self-motivated? Do they understand what marketable skills the must have? And most importantly, do they realize that now is the time to prepare?

THE SHIFT FROM OLD TO NEW WORK PLACE

Old ➔ New

Old	New
Supervisor holds authority	Workers have authority
Each worker performs single task; worker has single skill	Work teams, multi-skilled workers
Mass production	Adaptable production
Long production runs	Customized production runs
Worker stays with one company throughout career	Worker owns his own job, skills, career
Worker viewed as cost	Workers viewed as asset
Advancement based on seniority	Advancement based on documenting skills
Company accepts minimal qualifications	Company employs based on skills
Company offers workers minimal training	Company views training as essential for all workers
Narrow skills for some	Broader skills for all
Company dispenses information to decision makers	Company dispenses information to all
Little concern for foreign markets	Great attention to global economy
Remuneration based on title and degree	Remuneration based on degree of core skills

Adapted from Feller, Rich, and Gary Walz. 1996. *Career Transitions in Turbulent Times: Exploring Work, Learning, and Careers.* Greensboro, NC: ERIC-CASS.

The Importance of Career Development

Today's world forces our children to be flexible and adaptable in their lives/careers. They can adapt most successfully if they:

- learn to manage change
- discover what they love to do
- gain skills required to do it
- trust and appreciate themselves

Focus on the Future will help students to find direction in their lives. It will show them how education is relevant to their future goals and will motivate them to achieve. During the course, they will also learn decision-making and have a better understanding of career development as a lifelong process.

Effective Teaching Strategies

Focus on the Future is built on the principle that career development requires both information and insight. Teachers are familiar with providing information through lecture and discussion. We will use these pedagogical techniques in this course. However, students also need to reflect on the information so that they can apply it to their individual dreams and goals. By using such methods as brainstorming, role-playing, and small group activities you can help stimulate this insight.

Your students are also going through physical and psychological stages of development that affect the way in which they learn. For example, early adolescents are experiencing enormous physiological, physical, and psychological changes that cause them to shed the images of themselves as children and to test new identities.

Physiologically, young teens are going through the hormonal changes of puberty. The body they have come to know and trust is no longer the same. They are interested in the opposite sex, and relationships have new meaning. Their moods swing from one extreme to another. It is as if their emotions have short-circuited and they have no control.

Physically, they are developing the bodies that will identify them as adults. Unfortunately, growth is seldom steady or consistent. Girls tend to develop more quickly and often tower over boys in height. Growth is not even uniform in individuals. The feet and hands generally grow first, causing unbelievable clumsiness. Boys may fear that they will be midgets for the rest of their lives and girls are often uncomfortable with their developing breasts. Boys' voices are changing also and the cracking tones emitted can cause embarrassment. Young teens are often filled with restless energy and find it difficult to sit still.

Psychologically, feedback from their peers becomes very important as adolescents shape new concepts of their identities. They fear being different from their peers in the belief that they won't be accepted. Belonging to a group is very important. It assures them that they have a place in this strange new world between childhood and adulthood. Young adolescents tend not to be risk-takers unless they feel that the risk will give them status among their peers. Early adolescents are very egocentric, feeling that they are the center of the universe, and as such, are being observed and criticized at all times. They would rather say or do nothing than to risk being laughed at or appearing stupid. Young teens are also learning to be independent and to question the authority of their parents or other adults. They often rebel against being treated as "children."

You cannot reverse the characteristics of early adolescence. However, you can take advantage of them to enhance communication and to make your teaching strategies more effective. The activities in Focus on the Future allow students to socialize and learn from each other. They can use small groups to safely test new ideas and they can utilize play-acting to try out new roles without risking rejection from others. The curriculum uses the following teaching methods.

Teaching Methods[1]

1. Lecture: A lecture is a quick way for you to provide needed information, but it has its drawbacks. If you speak for too long and fail to involve the students, the class may become bored and restless—and ignore what you are teaching them.

2. Discussion: Discussions enable students to share their ideas, feelings, and thoughts about a specific subject. Pedagogically, discussions are particularly useful in helping students develop critical thinking. Discussions broaden and deepen students' understanding and give them the chance to apply what they have learned. You can use discussion groups of all sizes throughout this curriculum.

3. Brainstorming: Brainstorming encourages the free flow of ideas on a specific subject. You present a problem or issue and then encourage your students to suggest as many solutions and/or alternatives to the problem as they can. The group notes the recommendations without comment and evaluates them only after the suggestions stop. The class then evaluates each of the ideas.

4. Role-playing: During role-playing students assume a role in order to act out the various ways they can address a life situation. Role-playing helps students explore their feelings and thoughts in a safe environment in which they do not lose their privacy. Students should never be forced to role-play. Ask for volunteers and then teach some techniques to help them with the activity. For example, they can step out of character to tell others how they are feeling. You might also ask students to switch roles with their peers to generate new perspectives on the same situation. Role-playing is fun and encourages discussion.

5. Structured Activities: A structured activity is any planned experience that facilitates learning. It often simulates a life event in a controlled environment so that participants can observe and discuss it. This type of activity increases self-understanding in the presence of complicated life situations.

Teacher/Student Interaction

Teaching Exploring Future Options effectively depends on open lines of communication between and among participants. Your students need to understand and utilize basic rules of classroom discussion, while you must understand and utilize the basic interpersonal skills that facilitate group interaction. The following strategies will help both you and your students communicate effectively.

Classroom Discussion Rules for Students: Classroom discussions and activities run smoothly when everyone practices some basic rules. These include:

1. Listen to One Another: "Listening" means more than just hearing. When someone listens, they give thoughtful attention to what another person is saying. They maintain eye contact with the speaker and do not interrupt. When an individual finishes speaking, the next person gives a brief overview of what that individual has said before sharing her ideas.

---

1. Adapted from Shapiro, Susan. 1991. *Nutrition and your health*. New York: Open Society Institute.

2. Speak One at a Time: Only one person in a group may speak at a time. You might find it useful to have the speaker hold a symbol of authority, such as a gavel or a key, which she passes to the next speaker when she is finished. This tells everyone to listen to the individual because she has the floor. If other students carry on private conversations while an individual has the floor, stop the discussion until the designated speaker has everyone's full attention. Listening to one another and speaking one at a time are two rules that reinforce each other.

3. Stay on the Topic: Do not criticize a student who wanders from the topic. Rather, say: "Can you help me see how this relates to what we are talking about?" The student then has a chance to clarify his point or to recognize that his discussion is off topic.

4. Everyone's Ideas Are Important: You should encourage your students to express their thoughts and feelings freely. They should understand that their ideas are valuable and appreciated. If a student makes an inaccurate statement or repeats a myth, respond by saying, "Many people would agree with you. However, we now know that. . . ." This type of response prevents students from feeling embarrassed.

5. Right to Pass: Although you should encourage all students to participate in classroom activities, make sure that they know that they have the right to pass in situations in which participating might be embarrassing.

6. Outlaw Putdowns: Students will speak more freely if they understand that they can disagree with someone, but that they cannot attack or ridicule other people for their ideas. Help students to understand what putdowns sound like and how others feel when this type of behavior takes place. Let students know that you will not tolerate such behavior.

7. Questions Are Valued: Remind the students that there are no dumb questions. All questions are valuable. Let students know that you and the class will respect all questions and that you will answer whatever they ask.

Interpersonal Skills for Leaders: As an educator, you want to help your students develop and clarify their ideas and let them know that you understand what they are saying. You can facilitate helpful communications between you and your class and among your students by developing five interpersonal skills: listening, restating, clarifying, questioning, and seeking examples.

1. Listening: As we discussed above, listening means giving thoughtful attention to what someone is saying. It is an action-oriented activity that requires the use of all your senses. You can improve your ability to listen by paying attention to your students' verbal and nonverbal cues.

2. Restating: Restating is the process of repeating almost verbatim what another person has said. While restatement should be used sparingly, it provides you with an opportunity to make sure that you have heard a student correctly. You can also use restatement to let the student know that you have received her message.

3. Clarifying: Clarification enables you to help a student develop a new understanding of a topic based on the thoughts he has expressed. You might say, "During class you made the following point about ___. Let me see if I understand you correctly?" He then has the chance to agree or disagree with the new thought or idea you have advanced.

4. **Questioning:** When you are trying to understand a student's thoughts on a topic, using questions can be very helpful. However, use them sparingly and with caution. Here are a few tips on how to use them effectively:

   - **Ask open-ended questions.** "Could you tell me more? How did you feel? Is there anything else that you wish to say?"

   - **Ask only one question at a time.** Permit students to answer one question before moving on to another. Too many questions create confusion.

   - **Give the student an opportunity to answer the question.** Allow sufficient time if you believe that a student is thinking of an answer. Some students require time to think through a response.

   - **Validate the student's response.** Thank the student for participating. If the student has answered incorrectly, be positive when providing the correct answer.

   - **Give the student an out.** Watch for signs of agitation, fear, or an inability to respond. After a few moments of silence say, "You seem to be giving a lot of thought to my question. Would you like more time or would you like some help with the question?"

   - **End on a positive note.** Let students know that your questions were not easy and that they did a good job sharing their ideas.

5. **Seeking Examples:** Students often find it easier to use an example when trying to convey an abstract concept or idea. Simply asking "Could you give me an example or describe what you are trying to say?" will help them advance their thoughts.

By using all five interpersonal skills you will help your students expand on and develop their ideas. These communication skills keep conversations flowing. You can use them during classroom discussions, in activities, during role-plays, and in generating alternatives during decision-making.

FIVE INTERPERSONAL SKILLS TO FACILITATE COMMUNICATION

- **LISTENING**
- **RESTATING**
- **CLARIFYING**
- **QUESTIONING**
- **SEEKING EXAMPLES**

GROUP DYNAMICS

All groups go through four stages of development: forming, storming, norming, and performing. In new groups, participants are generally kind to each other and act with respect. However, as the group conducts its business, members typically will begin to disagree. This is normal; the group will usually work out its standards and will finally reach a level of productivity. However, there will be certain variables in the dynamics of any group that the leader will have to address. Having a plan to deal with these helps you become more effective. Some variables are:

- **Development of subgroups:** Subgroups are small clusters that form over time when you allow students to select their own groups in which to participate. These groups can be helpful because they enable students to develop a level of comfort that encourages group members to take more risks. However, subgroups also present problems. As students become more familiar with each other, they are less inclined to follow rules. One way of handling the problem is to form a variety of groups, varying their size and composition.

- **Opposing Groups:** Group members may divide into separate camps based on opposing points of view. If this happens, encourage the groups to accept each other's positions. Stress that while it is okay to disagree with one another, it is not okay to be disagreeable. Encourage students to focus on the issues instead of the positions.

- **Blaming:** Occasionally, students may openly attack individuals or subgroups for specific difficulties they experience. Blaming is very divisive because it breaks down trust, impedes progress, and isolates individuals. Stop the blaming immediately and emphasize that you will not tolerate it. Use the incident to teach the students how to apply the communication skills they have been learning to resolve their conflicts.

- **Monopolizing:** In their eagerness to contribute, some students may monopolize the session. When this happens, acknowledge their input but indicate that you want to involve everyone. Break eye contact with them and reduce the number of times that you call on them.

- **Inappropriate sharing:** If a student begins to talk about personal or very sensitive material that you believe should be private, step in immediately. Do so gently, acknowledging the student's feelings, but suggesting that she have this conversation with you after the session.

- **Silent members:** Many students tend to be rather quiet. This does not necessarily mean they are uninterested. Some people learn best by observing. Be ready to reach out to these youngsters, but also acknowledge their right to remain quiet.

- **Side conversations:** A small number of students may carry on their own conversation during class discussions. This can distract the group. Stop the conversation and ask these students to share their thoughts with the entire group. Remind them that the class cannot benefit from their ideas unless they share them with the entire group. Additionally, they cannot hear what others are saying if they are engaged in a private conversation. Review the rules for group discussion and move on.

- **Failure to stick with the topic:** Occasionally, a student will say something that is not related to the subject. Stop him and ask how what he is saying relates to the topic under discussion. This gives the student an opportunity to explain how his point is relevant or to acknowledge that what he said is unrelated. If his point is unrelated, ask him to either discuss it with you privately or to bring it up after the present discussion has ended.

- **Group discomfort:** Sometimes you may sense some discomfort in the group but are unable to identify what is happening. When this occurs, acknowledge your feelings and ask for their input. For example, you may say, "The group seems very quiet today. Can you help me understand what is happening?"

Most groups function well, and students enjoy discussions and activities that pertain to their futures. However, you must be sensitive to the group's dynamics. This will enhance learning and make it easier for students to address their needs.

ABOUT THE CURRICULUM

Exploring Future Options is designed to be user friendly. Each lesson plan contains all the information you need for the activity. However, in Unit Two, you will need to use other resources to help students find current labor market information. Government agencies, daily newspapers and the Internet are all useful. Labor market information is all around us. We just need to open our ears and eyes to its importance.

Because career development is a growth process that is very individual, we recommend that you do not grade students. Passing or failing students, or evaluating them on participation will only hurt them. They should understand that what they do can affect their future and that they are responsible for making the most of the course. The curriculum offers them an opportunity to learn about themselves and how their academic and vocational development affects their ability to live the lifestyle they want. We cannot control all the events that affect our choice of occupation. Nevertheless we must plan and give direction to our efforts. David Campbell wrote a book entitled *If You Don't Know Where You Are Going, You Will Probably End Up Somewhere Else* (Ave Maria Press, 1990). This might be the theme for educational and career-planning.

We have included a test of career development knowledge at the beginning of the curriculum. You can use this both before and after completing the curriculum to measure the knowledge your students have gained. The test is useful both as an individual measure of growth and as a group measure to see which lessons the students have learned well and which areas need reinforcement. Make sure that your students understand that they will retake the test at the end of the curriculum so that they can assess their own progress in learning about career development and in developing decision-making skills. Their ultimate indicator of success will be their understanding of the career opportunities open to them and the preparation they need to pursue their goals.

Exploring Future Options is divided into three units, each of which helps students to answer one of the critical questions of career development.

- **Unit One: Self-Knowledge** helps students investigate their interests, abilities, values, and dreams and learn how they relate to career development.

- **Unit Two: Career Exploration** helps students explore where they are going. What career opportunities are available to them after they have finished their formal education? How can they learn about different occupations?

- **Unit Three: Career-Planning** helps students to discover what educational and occupational preparation is required to pursue the career of their choice. What do they need to do to make their vision a reality?

At the beginning of each unit, there will be background information applicable to the lessons presented. Teachers are urged to use other available information to enhance the lessons. However, the background information presented will suffice to answer most questions.

Each unit begins with background information related to the lessons in that section. We urge you to use other available information to enhance the lessons. However, the background information we present will answer most questions.

Each unit consists of 12 sessions. Each session is divided into activity and discussion portions. We have broken the sessions down further into key instructional elements:

- OVERVIEW
- DURATION
- (Learning) OBJECTIVES
- MATERIALS NEEDED
- PREPARATION
- (Step-by-Step Guide to the) ACTIVITY

Most sessions also include discussion questions and one or more optional activities. The lesson durations we give are only suggestions. Allow time for teachable moments when you want to expand the lesson. We have designed the program to be flexible so that you can use your creativity, experience, and knowledge to adapt it to the specific needs of your students.

Parents will exert the most influence on their child's career choice. Therefore, you must encourage them to become involved in the activities in the curriculum and to be open to their children's questions. We have included "A Parent's Guide to Career Decision-Making" to help you explain the program and to show them how they can become involved.

We use Icons throuhout the curriculum to alert you to the following tasks.

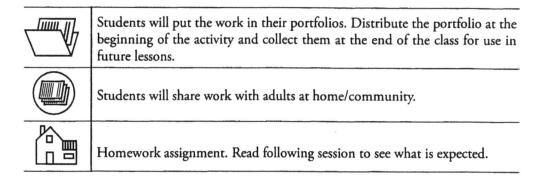

	Students will put the work in their portfolios. Distribute the portfolio at the beginning of the activity and collect them at the end of the class for use in future lessons.
	Students will share work with adults at home/community.
	Homework assignment. Read following session to see what is expected.

Each unit ends with a checklist of competencies that students should have attained from participating in the activities. The checklist is for self-assessment so that students can measure their progress and identify areas in which they may need more help.

If you gave the test of career development knowledge at the beginning of the program, you should repeat it at the end so that you can measure individual student growth and identify group strengths and weaknesses.

STUDENT PORTFOLIO

WHAT IS A PORTFOLIO?

A portfolio serves two functions. First, it provides a place for students to store their work during the course. Second, it helps students to see their progress and to reflect on the career development process. It should contain a student's best and most current work. The portfolio is a means for developing self-knowledge, not for educational assessment. It documents a student's thinking during the program so that she can refer to it in the future. Therefore, it belongs to the student.

We have students construct their portfolios at the beginning of Unit Three. However, there are certain optional activities in the first two units that are appropriate for the portfolios. If you choose to include these activities, you will want your students to construct their portfolios earlier.

 When you see this icon in the lesson plan, ask students to put this work in their portfolios. Keep the portfolios at school during the course so that they are readily available. At the end of the program, give the students their portfolios for future reference.

PART II
The Curriculum

∞

• UNIT ONE: SELF-KNOWLEDGE
Who Am I?

Unit One: Self-Knowledge
Who Am I?

This unit is designed to help students focus on the most important part of career decision-making: the person making those decisions. If students are to understand the concept of "Career as Life," they must appreciate the notion that they are in charge of that life and self-knowledge is a key to defining priorities and creating opportunities that will enhance that life.

Early adolescence is often a time of confusion and anxiety for teenagers as they struggle to define their identities. It is a critical time for schools to provide learning experiences that help adolescents sort out some of the confusion and reduce some of the anxiety. By focusing on self-knowledge, the career development curriculum attends to various facets of the developing individual and assists in defining the significant attributes that will help adolescents not only survive this turbulent time in their lives, but also to feel confident about their future.

One of the nice things about focusing on self-knowledge during these early adolescent years is that students often find comfort in the knowledge that they are not alone in their anxieties about who they are and where they're going. By sharing their thoughts, their dreams, and their concerns with each other and significant adults, they can be reassured that they are experiencing normal developmental impatience with the complex process of becoming mature adults.

The initial lesson in this unit introduces students to the purpose and scope of the *Exploring Future Options* curriculum. The teacher's role in setting the tone for the students' investment in and commitment to this curriculum will be critical during this first lesson. Try to emphasize how the career development curriculum is designed to link academic course requirements with a practical look at an ever-changing world economy. Even more important, stress how each student must assume responsibility for their own career choices. This may be an opportune time to share some personal examples of how choices you have made in the past have influenced your career journey.

The rest of the lessons in Unit One provide a general introduction to some of the many facets of the individual self. The earlier lessons begin with a look at the unique self, how achievement in school is an indication of the progress students are making, how they use their leisure time, and one even gives them permission to daydream (about their future). One lesson attends to the significant influence of families on students' career choices. Other lessons help students look at their unique ways of making decisions, coping with change, learning new information, and integrating their life experiences. Throughout this unit, it will be important to stress how Self-Knowledge is a life-long process of discovery, reflection, and integration. These lessons are just the beginning of the process.

SESSION 1:
INTRODUCTION TO *EXPLORING FUTURE OPTIONS*

OVERVIEW

Students learn about the *Exploring Future Options* curriculum and complete a questionnaire that measures their understanding of career development concepts.

DURATION

Approximately 30–45 minutes

OBJECTIVE

Students will be able to explain the purpose of the *Exploring Future Options* curriculum.

MATERIALS

Any materials that show the kinds of activities that students can expect as part of the *Exploring Future Options* curriculum

Discussion Rules (copies for each student)

What I Know About Career Decision-Making (copies for each student)

File folders and colored paper for constructing portfolios

PREPARATION

1. Read Part 1: Teacher's Guide. Review the lessons in the *Exploring Future Options* curriculum so you will be familiar with their content and can respond to students' questions.

2. Prepare a 5–10 minute summary of the *Exploring Future Options* curriculum, highlighting the topics and lessons.

ACTIVITY

1. Have students offer definitions of the term *readiness*. (Dictionary definition: prepared mentally or physically for some experience or action.)

2. Explain that they are beginning a new career development curriculum. This program will only be successful if they are ready to:

   a. look at themselves and their development;

   b. remain open to new learning opportunities;

   c. take some risks in exploring their futures.

3. Give them the 5–10 minute summary of the *Exploring Future Options* curriculum you have prepared and encourage them to find ideas and topics that will help them develop the readiness and motivation to stay focused for future lessons.

4. Write the words *awareness, exploration,* and *preparation* on the board. Explain that people who have a choice about their careers usually go through these three stages of development before they can fulfill their dreams. The *Exploring Future Options* curriculum will primarily focus on the awareness and exploration stages, but will also provide a framework for preparation that should serve them well during their remaining school years.

5. Respond to students' questions about the program.

6. Distribute Discussion Rules and explain that these rules will be guiding the class.

7. Ask students if they have ever heard of a portfolio. Talk about how artists use portfolios to collect and demonstrate what represents their best work. Tell students that they will also be using a portfolio to collect and retrieve information about themselves that they will use for career decision-making and job success. You will be holding their portfolios for safekeeping during the course, but students will take them home after the curriculum is completed.

8. Distribute the materials needed to construct the portfolio and explain how to make it. (Use the instructions on p. 131.)

9. Distribute What I Know About Career Decision-Making. Explain that there are no wrong answers as long as students respond honestly to each item. Have students individually complete the questionnaires.

10. When students have finished, review their answers and explain that they will complete the questionnaire again after they have participated in all the *Exploring Future Options* lessons.

DISCUSSION

1. Why should you begin working on career development issues at such a young age?

2. What are the benefits of a career development program for you? For the community? For the country?

3. Who is ultimately responsible for people's career success?

4. How can you demonstrate your readiness for learning career lessons that will help you later in life?

DISCUSSION RULES

1. **Listen to One Another:** Look at the speaker and listen to what she is saying. If it is your turn to speak, summarize what the previous person has said before contributing your ideas.

2. **Speak One at a Time:** Do not interrupt a speaker or talk while he is speaking.

3. **Stay on the Topic:** Make sure that you don't wander from the main point of discussion. If you think a fellow student is wandering, say, "I'm not sure how this relates to what we are talking about. Can you help me?"

4. **Everyone's Ideas Are Important:** Everyone in the class has value and is free to express feelings or thoughts. Never make fun of a person's ideas.

5. **Right to Pass:** You are encouraged to participate in the classroom discussions, but you can pass in those situations when you might feel embarrassed.

6. **No Putdowns:** You can disagree with someone, but don't judge other people for their ideas.

7. **Questions Are Valued:** There are no dumb questions. We must respect and answer all questions.

WHAT I KNOW ABOUT CAREER DECISION-MAKING
(TEACHER EDITION)

Instructions: Put an X under one of the columns to indicate whether you agree or disagree with a statement or if you just don't know.

STATEMENT	AGREE	DISAGREE	DON'T KNOW
1. Hobbies and leisure activities can be related to career interests.	X		
2. There is only one right way to make a decision.		X	
3. Whatever I choose for an occupation I am stuck with for the rest of my life.		X	
4. Career decision-making has nothing to do with the subjects I study in middle school.		X	
5. My performance in school can influence my success in life.	X		
6. I have considerable power over the changes that take place in my life.	X		
7. My personality has nothing to do with whether or not I am successful in my career.		X	
8. My family can be influential in my career choices.	X		
9. An occupation is different from an industry.	X		
10. Everyone learns in the same way, so if I am having difficulty learning something, it just means I am not trying hard enough.		X	
11. When making career decisions, people should consider other important roles they will play in life besides that of a worker.	X		
12. Work habits are developed once you get a job.		X	
13. One of the competencies that is expected of workers in modern society is the ability to work in teams.	X		

Statement	Agree	Disagree	Don't Know
14. My self-concept has nothing to do with my ability to make good decisions.		X	
15. It is all right to fantasize about the "perfect job," even though there will probably be many obstacles that would prevent me from ever ending up in that occupation.	X		
16. Career-planning can be a very complex process.	X		
17. I could benefit from learning about the mistakes and successes of others who have made career decisions.	X		
18. Older people have an advantage because they don't have to learn all the things that students do anymore.		X	
19. Who you know is often as important as what you know when it comes to getting a job.	X		
20. If I follow a step-by-step career decision-making model now, I will never have to use it again in the future because I will have done it right the first time.		X	

WHAT I KNOW ABOUT CAREER DECISION-MAKING

NAME:_____

DATE:_____

STATEMENT	AGREE	DISAGREE	DON'T KNOW
1. Hobbies and leisure activities can be related to career interests.			
2. There is only one right way to make a decision.			
3. Whatever I choose for an occupation I am stuck with for the rest of my life.			
4. Career decision-making has nothing to do with the subjects I study in middle school.			
5. My performance in school can influence my success in life.			
6. I have considerable power over the changes that take place in my life.			
7. My personality has nothing to do with whether or not I am successful in my career.			
8. My family can be influential in my career choices.			
9. An occupation is different from an industry.			
10. Everyone learns in the same way, so if I am having difficulty learning something, it just means I am not trying hard enough.			
11. When making career decisions, people should consider other important roles they will play in life besides that of a worker.			
12. Work habits are developed once you get a job.			
13. One of the competencies that is expected of workers in modern society is the ability to work in teams.			

STATEMENT	AGREE	DISAGREE	DON'T KNOW
14. My self-concept has nothing to do with my ability to make good decisions.			
15. It is all right to fantasize about the "perfect job," even though there will probably be many obstacles that would prevent me from ever ending up in that occupation.			
16. Career-planning can be a very complex process.			
17. I could benefit from learning about the mistakes and successes of others who have made career decisions.			
18. Older people have an advantage because they don't have to learn all the things that students do anymore.			
19. Who you know is often as important as what you know when it comes to getting a job.			
20. If I follow a step-by-step career decision-making model now, I will never have to use it again in the future because I will have done it right the first time.			

SESSION 2:
I Am Unique

OVERVIEW

We use a vocabulary lesson to demonstrate many of the facets of self-knowledge that students can examine as they begin the process of career exploration. A group story-telling activity weaves the vocabulary words into a conceptual synthesis of self-knowledge.

DURATION

Approximately 30 minutes

OBJECTIVES

1. Students will be able to define terms that are often applied in self-knowledge exercises for career decision-making.

2. Groups of students will be able to create stories that demonstrate their comprehension and application of self-knowledge/career development vocabulary.

MATERIALS

I Am Unique activity sheet (copies for each student)
Dictionaries for each small group

PREPARATION

None

ACTIVITY

1. Explain that today's lesson will help students develop the necessary vocabulary for taking a good look at themselves. Since self-knowledge is such an important part of career decision-making, they must look at their own unique characteristics and use this information for pursuing satisfactory careers.

2. Help the class come to a definition of self-knowledge.

3. In small groups of four to six, have students look up definitions of the terms on the activity sheet. (Have them take turns looking up words so that each group member makes a contribution.) Make sure they find definitions that are compatible with the concept of self-knowledge. Tell each group to discuss the definitions and come to an agreement that their definitions will help them explore self-knowledge.

4. Have groups develop cohesive stories that appropriately include all the vocabulary words. Make sure they have used the terms correctly.

DISCUSSION

1. How can a vocabulary lesson contribute to self-knowledge?

2. In what ways should people use self-knowledge for helping them with career decisions?

3. Is there ever a time when we outgrow the need for self-knowledge?

4. Are there other terms that we should explore in gaining self-knowledge?

5. In what ways might a lack of self-knowledge contribute to problems in a person's career?

OPTIONAL ACTIVITIES

1. If time allows, have someone from each group read his story to the rest of the class. Compare and contrast the stories.

2. Enlarge one of the better stories and use it as a bulletin board in the class. In later lessons on self-knowledge, use the bulletin board as a point of reference for integrating students' learning.

I Am Unique

PART 1:

Instructions:

Write the definitions of the following terms on the activity sheet. Be sure that the definition you choose is related to self-knowledge.

Achievement:

Aptitude:

Asset:

Competency:

Interest:

Knowledge:

Personality:

Role:

Trait:

Value:

PART 2:
Instructions:

Write a story using the words above. Underline these words in your text.

SESSION 3:
How Am I Doing?

OVERVIEW

Students will use an assessment of their progress in school to explore the impact of one's education on future career options.

DURATION

Approximately 30 minutes

OBJECTIVES

1. Students will be able to describe how their performance in school can have an influence on future career options.

2. Students will be able to assess their current strengths and challenges in academic areas.

MATERIALS

How Am I Doing? activity sheet (copies for each student)

PREPARATION

None

ACTIVITY

1. Explain that today's lesson focuses on how people's perceptions of their competence influences their career choices. Young adolescents often make judgments about their abilities based on how well they are doing in school. Ask them whether their past or current performance influences how well they do in the future. If so, how?

2. Distribute How Am I Doing? activity sheets. Have students list all the subjects they have studied in school. Next to each subject, have them place one of the following codes based on their estimation of how competent they are in that subject area:

   A = Highly Competent

   S = Satisfactory

   M = Major challenge

3. Have students put an * next to any subject in which they think they have the potential to do better now that they are more mature.

DISCUSSION

1. Why is it important to assess your overall progress in school, as well as your progress in individual subject areas?

2. How does your performance in school influence your perceptions of yourself?

3. If you are finding a subject particularly challenging, what actions can you take to improve?

4. How is academic success related to career success?

5. Besides academics, what other areas of success contribute to career success?

OPTIONAL ACTIVITY

Have students create action plans for improving their performance in academic subjects that are particularly challenging. Monitor their progress in meeting their goals.

ACTIVITY SHEET
HOW AM I DOING?

Name: _____

Instructions:

1. List all of the subjects you have studied in school in the table below.

2. Next to each subject place one of the letters:

      A = Highly Competent

      S = Satisfactory

      M = Major Challenge

based on how competent you think you are in the subject.

3. Place an * next to any subject in which you think you have the potential to improve.

SUBJECT	COMPETENCE	POTENTIAL TO DO BETTER
	A = Highly Competent S = Satisfactory M = Major Challenge	

SESSION 4:
IN MY SPARE TIME

OVERVIEW

Students will explore how hobbies or involvement in leisure activities can contribute to a successful life.

DURATION

Approximately 30 minutes, with some additional time spent outside class

OBJECTIVES

1. Students will be able to explain how leisure activities and hobbies contribute to a satisfying life.

2. Students will be able to name at least five hobbies or activities that they find personally enjoyable.

3. Students will be able to distinguish between those hobbies and activities that offer occupational possibilities and those that would be less satisfying if they were linked to their occupations.

MATERIALS

In My Spare Time activity sheet (copies for each student)

PREPARATION

None

ACTIVITY

1. Divide students into groups of five or six. Give them 10 minutes to brainstorm a list of things people can do as hobbies or as purposeful leisure activities. Encourage them to make the longest list possible. Make sure each group designates a recorder who writes down the suggestions. After 10 minutes, have each group share 10 hobbies or activities from their list.

2. Distribute In My Spare Time activity sheets. Have students list five hobbies or activities that they find most satisfying or rewarding. Tell them to put an "X" next to any hobby or activity in which they could see themselves being involved as an occupation. Have them share their list with others in their small group.

DISCUSSION

1. In what ways can hobbies or leisure activities contribute to a person's level of satisfaction in life?

2. What happens when people don't have things to do in their spare time?

3. What are some drawbacks to pursuing occupations that are closely linked to your hobbies and other leisure interests?

4. Do hobbies and other leisure activities have to cost a lot of money to be fun or rewarding?

5. What are some important lessons we can learn about career development from our involvement with hobbies and planned leisure activities?

OPTIONAL ACTIVITIES

1. Have students interview adults and ask them about the role of leisure in their lives.

2. Have students identify hobbies in which they are not involved currently but would like to be in the future. Have them develop a plan for pursuing the hobby.

IN MY SPARE TIME

Name: _____

Instructions:

1. List 5 hobbies or activities you enjoy.

2. Put an "X" next to any in which you can see yourself being involved as an occupation.

	HOBBY OR ACTIVITY	POSSIBLE OCCUPATION?
1		
2		
3		
4		
5		

SESSION 5:
WHEN IT'S OK TO DAYDREAM

OVERVIEW

Students are encouraged to daydream in order to free their minds to think about possible future goals. They will also explore how they can change career dreams.

DURATION

Approximately 30 minutes

OBJECTIVES

1. Students will be able to articulate their dreams for themselves when they are not limited by restrictions.

2. Students will be able to identify the negative and positive factors that contribute to altering one's career dreams.

MATERIALS

My World at 25 activity sheet (copies for each student)

PREPARATION

None

ACTIVITY

1. Have students recall a really good dream they had recently. (Some probably won't be able to recall one.) Have a few students share what their dreams were about (without giving too many details). Ask students, "What makes a good dream?" List their responses on the board.

2. Tell them that they have permission to daydream in this session and that for the next five minutes you would like the room to be perfectly quiet. During that time, they should free their minds to daydream about something wonderful happening to them. After five minutes, ask students jot down a few statements that explain why their dreams were wonderful.

3. Distribute My World at 25 activity sheets and tell the students that you want them to day-dream about how they would like to see themselves when they are 25 years old. Be sure to emphasize that this is a "good" dream. Where do they live in this dream world? What kind of work do they do? What are the other things in their world that make this a good dream? After about 5 minutes, ask them to record as many details as possible about their future dream world. Be sure they name the kind of jobs they pictured.

4. Ask students to write a paragraph about a day in their future world.

DISCUSSION

1. What are the benefits of daydreaming about the future?

2. What are some of the negative factors in people's lives that keep them from pursuing their dreams?

3. What are some of the positive factors in people's lives that can help them attain their dreams?

4. Should people entirely abandon their dreams because of life's realities? If not, how can people create alternative dreams that are probably not ideal, but are still good ones?

OPTIONAL ACTIVITY

Have students create drawings that represent their daydreams about the future. Display the drawings and use them as a focus for a discussion about future aspirations and the kinds of challenges young people face in pursuing their dreams.

HOMEWORK ALERT

Distribute Family Connections activity sheets from Session 6 and review with your students. Ask them to complete Part 1 of the sheet for as many members of their extended family as possible.

Note: For some family members, the statements might be derived from conversations with parents or other relatives who knew the people well, since it may not be possible to directly contact each individual. It may also be plausible to make statements about deceased relatives about whom family members have sufficient information to draw these conclusions.

MY WORLD AT 25

Name: _____

PART 1:

Instructions:

Daydream about how you would like your world to be when you are 25 and answer the following questions.

1. WHERE DO I LIVE (town, city, country)**?**

2. WHAT KIND OF WORK DO I DO (writing, problem-solving, working with machines, computers, people)**?**

3. HOW DO I SPEND MY LEISURE TIME?

PART 2:

Instructions:

Write a paragraph description of a day in your life based on the answers to these questions.

SESSION 6:
FAMILY CONNECTIONS

OVERVIEW

Students will identify the occupations of members of their extended families and use this information to draw conclusions about how families influence life/career decisions.

DURATION

Students will spend 1–2 hours at home investigating information about their extended families. In-class time should take 30–45 minutes.

OBJECTIVES

1. Students will be able to identify themes about job/occupational satisfaction from investigating family members' work experiences.

2. Students will be able to draw conclusions about their future career initiatives based on insights gained from investigating family members' work experiences.

MATERIALS

Family Connections activity sheet (multiple copies for each student)

PREPARATION

Make sure students have completed Part 1 of their Family Connections activity sheets.

ACTIVITY

1. Explain that today's session is designed to help students understand and appreciate the many lessons about career development that they can learn from family members. Students have the choice of learning form and modeling work behavior or finding new directions based on the lessons learned.

2. Have students individually look over their lists and do the following tasks:

   a. Group the jobs that are similar. (Categories might be "Manual Labor," "Clerical Jobs," "Working with Numbers," etc.)

b. Put stars next to the two statements that seem to provide the most important messages about career satisfaction.

c. In two or three sentences, draw some conclusions about their families' work experiences and the messages that seem important for career decision-making.

3. In small groups of four to six, have students share information about what they have discovered. Encourage them to listen to others' reflections and compare and contrast the different perspectives.

DISCUSSION

1. Why is it important to listen to and learn from your family when exploring the world of work?

2. How can information from this simple investigation influence your future career choices?

3. If you were to summarize what you have learned from this lesson in one sentence, what would it be?

FAMILY CONNECTIONS

PART 1:

Instructions:

Complete this short survey for each member of your extended family that you can contact.

NAME OF FAMILY MEMBER:

OCCUPATION:

WAS JOB ENJOYABLE OR REWARDING? _____ YES _____ NO

HOW MY RELATIVE FELT ABOUT HIS/HER WORK:

_____

NAME OF FAMILY MEMBER:

OCCUPATION:

WAS JOB ENJOYABLE OR REWARDING? _____ YES _____ NO

HOW MY RELATIVE FELT ABOUT HIS/HER WORK:

_____

NAME OF FAMILY MEMBER:

OCCUPATION:

WAS JOB ENJOYABLE OR REWARDING? _____YES _____NO

HOW MY RELATIVE FELT ABOUT HIS/HER WORK:

NAME OF FAMILY MEMBER:

OCCUPATION:

WAS JOB ENJOYABLE OR REWARDING? _____YES _____NO

HOW MY RELATIVE FELT ABOUT HIS/HER WORK:

PART 2:

Instructions:

Look over your list and complete the following tasks:

1. Group the jobs that are similar. (Categories might be "Manual Labor," "Clerical Jobs," "Working with Numbers," etc.)

2. Put stars next to the two statements that seem to provide the most important messages about career satisfaction.

3. In two or three sentences, draw some conclusions about your family's work experiences and the messages that seem important for career decision-making.

SESSION 7:
DECISION-MAKING BY THE NUMBERS

OVERVIEW

A mathematical model of decision-making will lead to a discussion about personal styles of decision-making.

DURATION

Approximately 30–45 minutes

OBJECTIVES

1. Students will be able to employ a mathematical model of decision-making for addressing a significant school-based or personal issue.

2. Students will be able to explain their personal models of decision-making.

MATERIALS

Decision-Making by the Numbers sample (copies for each student)
Decision-Making by the Numbers activity sheet (copies for each student)

PREPARATION

Be sure to go over the directions to the mathematical decision-making model to make sure you understand them and can use the model with the various decisions students make.

ACTIVITY

1. Distribute copies of Decision-Making by the Numbers samples and activity sheets. Explain that today the class will be talking about decision-making. When it comes to making career choices, the actual act of making a decision is where many people get "stuck."

2. For this lesson, students will be using a mathematical/logical model of decision-making. Other more intuitive models will be explored later.

3. Here's how the mathematical model works:

   a. Have students identify a significant decision that they must make (e.g., where to go to the movies, choosing the theme for a school dance, etc.). Write the decision in the appropriate place on the activity sheet.

   b. Ask them to list the alternatives in the appropriate boxes on the activity sheet. (Try to have more than two, if possible, so the decision does not seem so "black-and-white.")

   c. Brainstorm all the values that should be considered as a part of the decision (e.g., costs, health issues, respect, environment, fun, risk, etc.).

   d. Place the values in rank order based on personal priorities in the "Values" column.

   e. Assign each value a score from 1–10, with 10 being assigned to the most important value, then 9 for the next most important value, and so on down to 1 which is assigned to the least important value. It is all right to skip a number when there is a large discrepancy between one value and the next one. Write that value in the "Value Rating" column.

   f. Go back to the alternatives and rate each one in comparison to the listed values. Insert the rating in the appropriate column of the "Favorability Scale." If a particular alternative favorably addresses the value in every way, it receives a 2. If it meets the value in most ways, but has some drawbacks, it receives a 1. If it seems pretty neutral in the way it meets values, give it a 0. If it has more drawbacks than positive ways of complementing the value, give it a -1. If it in no way addresses the value and is seen as a total negative, give it a -2.

   g. Multiply the Favorability Score by the Value Rating and place the number in the appropriate column.

   h. Add the columns under each alternative.

   i. Decide whether the alternative with the highest score is the best alternative.

   j. The most important part of the decision-making model is the decision that it generates since the value ratings and favorability scores may change depending on the circumstances.

DISCUSSION

1. How many people liked this model of decision-making? How many didn't like it? Why do some people prefer a more logical process of decision-making while others trust themselves to make decisions that "feel" right?

2. What did you learn about decision-making from this lesson?

3. What are some examples of times when you wish you had been more logical in your decision-making?

4. How do people use decision-making in work situations?

5. How is decision-making related to career development?

OPTIONAL ACTIVITY

As a language arts/writing assignment, have each student write a paragraph explaining his or her personal decision-making model.

HOMEWORK ALERT

Distribute copies of Making Change activity sheets from Session 8 and review. Ask students to complete it as a homework assignment.

SAMPLE:

DECISION-MAKING BY THE NUMBERS

VALUE SCALE

FAVORABILITY SCALE

Values	Rating	Alternative 1: Disneyland		Alternative 2: Wild West Ranch		Alternative 3: Boy Scout Camp	
		Favorability Score	Favorability Score x Value Rating	Favorability Score	Favorability Score x Value Rating	Favorability Score	Favorability Score x Value Rating
Cost	10	-1	-10	0	0	1	10
Fun	9	2	18	2	18	2	18
Varied activities	7	1	7	0	0	2	14
Good food	5	1	5	2	10	-1	-5
Good accommodations	3	0	0	2	6	0	0
Good weather	1	2	2	2	2	1	1
TOTAL			22		36		38

PRIORITY SCALE	
10 = HIGHEST PRIORITY	
1 = LOWEST PRIORITY	

FAVORABILITY SCALE	
Addresses the value in every way	2
Meets the value in most ways but has some drawbacks	1
Neutral in the way it meets the value	0
More drawbacks than positive ways of meeting the value	-1
Does not address the value	-2

DECISION-MAKING BY YHE NUMBERS

Instructions:

There are many ways to make a decision. One way is to use a mathematical/logical model in which you use numbers to rank values and evaluate alternatives. Here's how it works:

1. Identify a significant decision that you must make (e.g., where to go with your friends, choosing the theme for a school dance, etc.).

2. List the alternatives in the appropriate boxes on the activity sheet. (Try to have more than two, if possible.)

3. Brainstorm all the values that should be considered as a part of the decision (e.g., costs, health issues, respect, environment, fun, risk, etc.).

4. Based on your personal priorities, place the values in rank order in the "Values" column.

5. Assign each value a score from 1–10, with 10 being assigned to the most important value and 1 being assigned to the least. You may skip a number when there is a large discrepancy between one value and the next one. Write that value in the "Value Rating" column.

6. Now rate each alternative in terms of the listed values and insert the rating in the appropriate column of the "Favorability Scale." If a particular alternative meets the value in every way, give it a 2. If it meets the value in most ways, but has some drawbacks, give it a 1. If it seems pretty neutral in the way it meets values give it a 0. If it has more drawbacks than positive ways of complementing the value, give it a -1. If it doesn't meet the value at all, give it a -2. Refer to the sample activity sheet to see how this is done.

7. Multiply the Favorability Score by the Value Rating and place the number in the appropriate column.

8. Add the columns under each alternative.

9. Decide whether the alternative with the highest score is the best alternative.

Decision-Making Model

Decision: _____

Value Scale

Values	Rating	Alternative 1: Disneyland		Alternative 2: Wild West Ranch		Alternative 3: Boy Scout Camp	
		Favorability Score	**Favorability Score x Value Rating**	**Favorability Score**	**Favorability Score x Value Rating**	**Favorability Score**	**Favorability Score x Value Rating**
Cost							
Fun							
Varied activities							
Good food							
Good accommodations							
Good weather							
TOTAL							

Priority Scale		Favorability Scale	
10 = HIGHEST PRIORITY		Addresses the value in every way	2
1 = LOWEST PRIORITY		Meets the value in most ways but has some drawbacks	1
		Neutral in the way it meets the value	0
		More drawbacks than positive ways of meeting the value	-1
		Does not address the value	-2

2006 © Open Society Institute

The Publisher grants permission for the reproduction of this worksheet for non-profit educational purposes only.
Activity sheets may be downloaded from www.idebate.org/conflictandcommunication.htm

SESSION 8:
MAKING CHANGE

OVERVIEW

A homework assignment encourages students to identify significant changes that are taking place in their lives. We use "making change" as a simile for looking at the process of change.

DURATION

Approximately 30 minutes, with a homework assignment preceding the lesson

OBJECTIVES

1. Students will be able to identify major changes taking place at the local, national, and international levels.

2. Students will be able to draw conclusions and generate implications about the nature of change in their world.

MATERIALS

Making Change activity sheet (copies for each student)

PREPARATION

1. Make sure that students have finished their homework assignment: completing Making Change activity sheets.

2. Before the class begins, divide the board into 3 sections and put one of the following headings at the top of each: LOCAL, NATIONAL, and INTERNATIONAL. Divide each major column in half, labeling the first half change and the second half *implication*.

ACTIVITY

1. Tell the students that the homework assignment they completed will be the focus of today's lesson. The ability to cope with change is a critical aspect of today's economy and job market. They need to understand their own personal challenges for embracing change.

2. Have students take turns putting information from their homework assignments on the board, avoiding duplication (or use another technique that is more manageable). Make sure they list their responses under the proper category.

3. Introduce the concept of a simile. (Dictionary definition: a figure of speech comparing two unlike things that is often introduced by *like* or *as*.) Ask students to think of ways that the changing world is like *making change*. (You may need to list their responses on chart paper if the board is already full of the list of changes.)

DISCUSSION

1. What are the implications for society when we look at the changes taking place in the world?

2. What are the implications for individuals if they are to be successful in a changing world?

3. How do you tell the difference between good change and bad change?

OPTIONAL ACTIVITY

Have students come to a consensus about "10 Major Implications of Change" that can be posted on the classroom wall. Have them think about how they will choose which implications get omitted from the list and which ones are retained.

MAKING CHANGE

Instructions:

1. Find out what major changes are taking place at the local, national, and international levels by watching television or listening to the radio and reading the newspapers.

2. List the changes on the table below.

3. Describe what you think the implications of each change will be.

LOCAL		NATIONAL		INTERNATIONAL	
CHANGE	IMPLICATION	CHANGE	IMPLICATION	CHANGE	IMPLICATION

SESSION 9:
LEARNING IN STYLE

OVERVIEW

Students will informally assess their learning styles and, in groups comprised of people with similar learning styles, create an advertisement that reflects their style.

DURATION

Approximately 30–45 minutes

OBJECTIVES

1. Students will be able to identify their learning style preference.

2. Students will be able to apply their learning style in a creative activity.

MATERIALS

Learning Styles resource sheet (copies for each student)
Some students may need colored paper, markers, or chart paper, depending on their choice of learning style.

PREPARATION

1. If you are not familiar with the literature on learning styles, it may be helpful to ask colleagues for information on the topic or request journal articles about the use of learning styles in the classroom. However, this lesson does not require any more than a cursory understanding of the concept.

2. Put the words AUDITORY, VISUAL, TOUCHING, and COMBINATION on the board.

ACTIVITY

1. Explain that today's lesson is about learning styles. A learning style is a preferred way of using one's abilities. There are many different ways that people choose to classify learning styles, but we're going to use a rather simple approach today.

2. Distribute copies of Learning Styles resource sheets and discuss.

3. Have students decide which of the four learning styles is the one they prefer.

4. Designate one corner of the room for each of the learning styles. Have students stand in one of the four corners of the room that corresponds to their learning style.

5. Tell the groups to develop a one-minute advertisement for a popular product (based on local preferences). All four groups will be advertising the SAME product. The advertisement should reflect their learning style preference. Give them 10–15 minutes to develop the advertisement.

6. Have the groups present their advertisements.

DISCUSSION

1. How did the advertisements reflect the different learning styles?

2. How can your knowledge of your learning style affect your ability to do homework?

3. How can your learning style affect your performance in school?

4. How does one's learning style contribute to job performance in the world of work?

  ## HOMEWORK ALERT

Distribute copies of Words of Wisdom activity sheets from Session 10. Tell students that they are to ask their parents or guardians to provide them with "words of wisdom" about the categories on the sheet. Parents may need two or three days to think about their responses.

LEARNING STYLES

FOUR TYPES OF LEARNING

AUDITORY: learns through verbal instructions, dialogue, recordings, music, and/or sounds.

VISUAL: learns by seeing, watching demonstrations, reading, writing, images, drawing, diagrams, and/or note-taking.

TOUCHING: learns by actively participating, handling, rhythmic body movement, gesturing, and/or other physical involvement.

COMBINATION: a fairly equal combination of the above three styles is necessary for maximum learning.

SESSION 10:
A STORY THAT MATTERS

OVERVIEW

Students will interview their parents or guardians, seeking "words of wisdom" about various aspects of life. They will then develop personal stories that integrate the messages.

DURATION

Approximately 30 minutes, with students spending additional time on homework assignments

OBJECTIVES

1. Students will be able to involve their parents or guardians in their life development.

2. Students will be able to produce a written piece that incorporates their parents' or guardians' messages into a meaningful "story that matters."

MATERIALS

Words of Wisdom activity sheet (copies for each student)

PREPARATION

1. Be sure that students have completed their Words of Wisdom activity sheets: ask their parents or guardians to provide them with "words of wisdom" about the categories on the sheet. Parents may need two or three days to think about their responses.

2. As part of your own preparation, think of a personal anecdote that illustrates how you have used an important message from your parents or guardians to help you in life.

3. Think about the kinds of compositions you want students to write. Should they be creative? Summative? Philosophical? Humorous? Any style they choose?

ACTIVITY

1. Introduce the lesson by sharing the anecdote about how your parents' message helped you in life. Tell students that the ultimate goal of this lesson is to help them generate the messages that will help them stay focused in life.

2. Have them spend the class time creating a composition that incorporates their parents' or guardians' messages into a "story that matters." Even if they disagree with a message that has been offered to them, they should find a way to honor the message while creating a different perspective for it. Their goal in writing the composition should be to shape an integrated story or theme that connects the various messages. Encourage them to ask for help from peers in looking at ways to link their story themes.

DISCUSSION

1. How did it feel to talk with your parents or guardians about these topics?

2. Where do our beliefs about such important aspects of our life development come from?

3. How can the stories we have developed help us when making career decisions?

OPTIONAL ACTIVITIES

1. Have students share their stories in small groups (but give them the option not to share if their stories are too personal). Have peers provide feedback and suggestions about ways to improve the stories or to think about them from different perspectives. Have the students refine their stories so they are considered their "best work."

2. Post the stories on the classroom wall or in the hallway (with students' permission). Give students time to read each others' compositions. Have the class identify the common themes or significant messages that emerge.

HOMEWORK ALERT

Have students summarize what they have learned about themselves from Sessions 2–10 of this self-knowledge unit. Have them limit the summary to four to five paragraphs so that they are challenged to integrate some of the lessons. Tell them their summaries will be included in their portfolios, so they should incorporate the kinds of messages they want others to know about them.

Adapted from "A Story that Matters" in Buchan, B.A. and Zark Van Zandt. 1997. *Lessons for Life: A Complete Career Development Activities Library.* West Nyack, NY: The Center for Applied Research in Education.

WORDS OF WISDOM

Instructions:

Ask your parents or guardians to provide you with "words of wisdom" (no more than one or two sentences) for each of the following categories:

MARRIAGE: _____
_____
_____
_____

FRIENDS: _____
_____
_____
_____

FAMILY: _____
_____
_____
_____

WORK: _____
_____
_____
_____

LEISURE: _____
_____
_____
_____

SPIRITUALITY: _____
_____
_____
_____

SESSION 11:
WHAT IT ALL COMES DOWN TO

OVERVIEW

This lesson allows students to summarize what they have learned about themselves in the previous self-knowledge lessons.

DURATION

Approximately 30–45 minutes

OBJECTIVES

1. Students will be able to explain how a "whole" can be greater than the sum of its "parts."

2. Students will be able to summarize what they have learned about themselves in the previous self-knowledge lessons.

3. Students will be able to explain how their personal "whole" is greater than the sum of their "parts."

MATERIALS

None

PREPARATION

1. As a homework assignment, have students summarize what they have learned about themselves from Sessions 2–10 of this self-knowledge unit. Have them limit the summary to four to five paragraphs so that they are challenged to integrate some of the lessons. Tell them their summaries will be included in their portfolios, so they should represent the kinds of messages they want others to know about them.

2. Think of examples to show how "the whole is greater than the sum of its parts," in case students have difficulty understanding the concept.

   Example: A bunch of gears, a couple wheels, some handlebars, a seat, and some pedals are individually quite impressive "parts." But when they are skillfully combined they become something even more significant than just a bunch of parts. High-quality materials and craftsmanship make the "whole" even more outstanding.

ACTIVITY

1. Ask students to come up with examples of how "the whole is greater than the sum of the parts." After four or five examples, explain that the homework assignment that asked them to summarize what they learned about themselves from Lessons 2–10 of the self-knowledge unit is designed to help them look at the "parts" that make up their unique selves.

2. For a minimum of 5 minutes, have students individually reflect and write down their thoughts about how they are much more than what they have summarized on paper.

3. In groups of four to five, have students share their reflections. Tell them to listen closely to what others in their groups are saying.

4. After they have had a chance to listen to each other, have them go back and individually revise and refine their statements about how they are more than the sum of their parts.

5. Have students add their revised statements to their portfolios.

DISCUSSION

1. How did this lesson help you think about who you are and how you can use this information for making career decisions?

2. What other kinds of information do you hope to find out about yourself in the coming years?

3. What have you discovered about the uniqueness of your friends and classmates?

OPTIONAL ACTIVITY

Have students add their revised statements to their portfolios.

SESSION 12:
Personal Portrait

OVERVIEW

This lesson asks students to think about what an artist should try to capture in a self-portrait. It then has students use their suggestions to generate ideas about what their self-portraits should try to capture.

DURATION

Approximately 30 minutes

OBJECTIVES

1. Students will be able to describe the tangible and intangible ingredients for a quality self-portrait.
2. Students will be able to apply their language and insights about self-portraits in describing themselves to others.

MATERIALS

None

PREPARATION

Both of the following suggestions will be helpful, but are not absolutely essential, in presenting the lesson:

1. If possible, find a picture of a famous artist who has drawn his or her self-portrait.
2. Talk with an art teacher or local artist who can share some of the terminology and techniques used in creating self-portraits.

ACTIVITY

1. Tell students about the picture you have chosen as an example of a self-portrait (or give a brief explanation about self-portraits).

2. Ask students to identify all the things they can think of that should go into the creation of a high-quality self-portrait. Write their ideas on the board.

3. Explain that when people enter a competitive job market, they will need to be able to describe themselves to best advantage and really make themselves look good—somewhat like painting a self-portrait.

4. Using as many phrases from the board as possible (but using them more as metaphors than as technical terms), have students brainstorm ways they can develop their own quality self-portraits.

DISCUSSION

1. What makes it difficult to create accurate and positive self-portraits?

2. What is the difference between self-confidence and arrogance?

3. If you're not satisfied with your self-portrait, what can you do to change it?

4. How should one's figurative "self-portrait" change over time?

OPTIONAL ACTIVITIES

1. Have students actually produce self-portraits. They shouldn't necessarily have to produce artwork, but they should try to be creative in finding ways to represent who they are and what they're like.

2. If students produce something of which they are particularly proud, encourage them to include it (or a description of it) in their portfolios.

Unit One:
Competency Checklist

As a result of my participation in Unit One, I ... (Check those items for which you feel you have attained competency.)

☐ ... understand why self-knowledge is important in career decision-making.

☐ ... appreciate how my unique traits and abilities can help me in my career.

☐ ... understand how my performance in school can influence my future career options.

☐ ... am more aware of my academic strengths and challenges.

☐ ... appreciate how leisure activities can contribute to a more satisfying life.

☐ ... know of some hobbies or leisure interests I want to pursue in the future.

☐ ... understand how my dreams for my future say something about what I think is important to me.

☐ ... am able to use advice and information from my family to help me focus on important issues in my own career development.

☐ ... can appreciate how different kinds of decisions may require different levels of time, energy, investigation, and commitment on my part.

☐ ... can use my own decision-making model to make important life decisions.

☐ ... understand my own learning style and how it affects my performance in school.

☐ ... appreciate how my family has shaped some of my beliefs about what matters in life.

☐ ... know many of the various parts that contribute to my knowledge of who I am and what matters to me.

☐ ... appreciate how I must continue to learn about myself for the rest of my life.

• UNIT TWO: CAREER EXPLORATION
Where Am I going?

UNIT TWO: CAREER EXPLORATION
WHERE AM I GOING?

In addition to self-knowledge, students also need to become knowledgeable about the world of work. The middle grades provide an opportune time for both awareness and exploration of the opportunities and challenges offered by the emerging world economy.

One of the most important messages students can learn about their career journey is that the process is more important than the choice. The reality of the work world in industrialized market economies is that typical adults make an average of 5 to 7 major career "shifts" during their working years. (A career shift does not necessarily mean changing to a completely different occupation, but it does connote a change that requires new educational or technical training on the part of the worker.) If students develop the skills and attitudes for conducting thorough and reflective searches of the world of work, they will feel confident in addressing similar searches in the future.

Career awareness should lay the foundation for career exploration. In this first stage of the career-development process, we need to open students' minds to the possibilities that are offered to them in the world of work. We also need to make them aware of the other life roles that will have an impact on their occupational choices. Without a sense of direction and perspective, the possibilities can be overwhelming to students. However, a program that helps them make sense of the world of work and provides a means of narrowing choices can shift students' affective responses from being overwhelmed to being motivated and anticipatory about their futures.

Career exploration is an exciting process because it allows people to dabble in an area for a while, eliminating options or investigating them further if they choose. There are few other areas in life that allow for such freedom to make mistakes and say "no" a lot, and still make progress! Knowing what they don't want is as important as identifying what they do want at this stage of their career development. The whole career exploration helps them define and refine their sense of where they want to go in life.

The lessons in Unit Two are focused on making sense of the world in which students live, while also "expanding their horizons" by introducing them to new opportunities and new perspectives that will help them adapt to an ever-changing society and global economy. Because this program may be students' first foray into career development lessons, it may be important to reinforce the notion that what they learn in these lessons will help prepare them for more advanced career exploration and planning in their high-school years. The seriousness with which they approach these lessons may contribute to their success in the higher grades and ultimately to their life satisfaction in adulthood. The process they learn for exploring and making life choices can be more powerful than any single choice they make in life. *If you give people fish, they eat for a day; if you teach them to fish, they eat for a lifetime.*

SESSION 13:
THE ART OF EXPLORING

OVERVIEW

Students will relate the process of exploring careers to the actions of explorers from history.

DURATION

Approximately 30 minutes

OBJECTIVES

1. Students will be able to describe the kinds of attributes that are necessary to be a good explorer.

2. Students will be able to identify personal attributes that will be either strengths or challenges in their own career explorations.

MATERIALS

Art of Exploring activity sheet (copies for each student)
Globe or map of the world, if available (not essential)

PREPARATION

Identify the explorers that students have studied in their history classes.

ACTIVITY

1. Using the globe or map, have the students point out some of the areas of the world that have been explored and name several people who have explored these regions.

2. Distribute Art of Exploring activity sheets. Have the class brainstorm a list of adjectives that are characteristic of explorers. Try to generate at least 20 adjectives and write them on the board. Once the list is complete, ask students to copy the adjectives onto the activity sheet.

3. Ask students to explain how career exploration requires some of the same traits (e.g., risk-taking is needed to investigate career options that are new or different).

4. Ask each student to review the list and choose three of the adjectives that they also possess as personal traits and insert them in the activity sheet. Then ask each student to choose two adjectives they wish they had because they believe them to be essential for achieving success in life. Ask them to write them on the activity sheet as well.

DISCUSSION

1. What are some important things to remember about career exploration?

2. What are some of the things you hope to explore about careers?

3. What are some of the challenges you will face as you explore your career options?

OPTIONAL ACTIVITIES

1. Have students generate phrases (e.g., "Navigating Our Future," "Finding Our Directions," "Discover What's Out There") that link exploration metaphors to the career exploration process. Create an attractive bulletin board that displays the phrases.

2. Have students write a short essay about how they can develop the two traits they have chosen to enhance their career journey.

THE ART OF EXPLORING

Instructions:

Brainstorm a list of adjectives that are characteristic of explorers and write them below.

20 ADJECTIVES THAT DESCRIBE EXPLORERS

1._____   11._____

2._____   12._____

3._____   13._____

4._____   14._____

5._____   15._____

6._____   16._____

7._____   17._____

8._____   18._____

9._____   19._____

10._____   20._____

Instructions:

Review the list above and choose three of the traits that you possess.

THE THREE TRAITS I POSSESS ARE:

1. _____

2. _____

3. _____

Instructions:

Choose two traits you wish you possessed.

THE TWO TRAITS I WISH I HAD ARE:

1. _____

2. _____

SESSION 14:
LIFE'S A PUZZLE

OVERVIEW

Students will examine five interconnecting life roles that are keys to understanding the concept of career.

DURATION

Approximately 30 minutes

OBJECTIVES

1. Students will be able to identify the five interconnecting life roles that influence their careers.

2. Students will be able to explain how balancing life roles is an important aspect of career satisfaction.

MATERIALS

Life Roles resource sheet (copies for each student)

Life's a Puzzle activity sheet (copies for each student)

Sheet of paper (of identical size) for each student. This can be scrap paper or newspaper.

Scissors (optional)

PREPARATION

1. Think about the percentage of time you spend in each life role. Be prepared to explain why some roles receive (deserve?) more attention than others.

2. After the initial brainstorming, write the following words on the board: WORK, LEISURE, CITIZEN, FAMILY, SPIRITUAL.

ACTIVITY

1. Distribute Life Roles resource sheets and discuss.

2. Distribute Life's a Puzzle activity sheets. Ask students to brainstorm all the roles they play daily (e.g., son/daughter, friend, ball player, etc.) and write them on the activity sheet. Generate a master list and put it on the board.

3. In small groups, have students sort the roles into the Five Life Roles categories (work, leisure, citizen, family, spiritual). See if the groups can agree about where the roles fit.

4. With each student supplied with a sheet of paper, have them cut or tear five pieces that represent the amount of time they spend playing each role on a weekly basis.

5. Take a poll to see which roles students think take up most of a person's life. Which ones take up the least amount of time and energy?

DISCUSSION

1. What was the purpose of this lesson?

2. How did your life roles compare with those of your friends and classmates?

3. Do you think good friends and family members would view your roles differently?

4. Do all life roles deserve equal time and commitment for your life to be balanced?

OPTIONAL ACTIVITY

Suggest to your students that they do the same activity with a sibling or parent.

Adapted from Buchan and VanZandt. 1997. *Lessons for Life: A Complete Career Development Activities Library.* West Nyack, NY: The Center for Applied Research in Education.

LIFE ROLES

Our "jobs" do not exist in isolation from the rest of our lives. We don't leave our "lives" behind in the morning when we go to work, and work is only one part of our life/career. We all have five interconnected life roles:

WORK: finding occupations that provide satisfaction and enough income to meet our responsibilities.

LEISURE: the way we choose to spend our time when the rest of life's demands have given us time of our own.

CITIZEN: the way we choose to participate in and contribute to our communities.

FAMILY: the choices we make to shape our family life. These include choosing life partners, determining the size of our family, nurturing special relationships, and celebrating important occasions.

SPIRITUAL: seeking experiences that help to "feed our soul."

LIFE'S A PUZZLE

Instructions:

Think of all the roles you play daily (e.g. son/daughter, friend, ball player, etc.). List the roles below.

ROLES I PLAY DAILY:

_____   _____
_____   _____
_____   _____
_____   _____

Instructions:

Sort your roles into the Five Life Roles categories below.

WORK	LEISURE	CITIZEN	FAMILY	SPIRITUAL

SESSION 15:
WORK STUDY

OVERVIEW

Students will discover how they are already developing work habits that will serve them in their future careers as well as in their present roles as students.

DURATION

Approximately 30 minutes

OBJECTIVES

1. Students will be able to analyze how work habits develop early in their lives.

2. Students will be able to list the employment skills gained by having various job responsibilities while they are in school.

MATERIALS

Work Study activity sheet (copies for each student)

PREPARATION

Think of your own work experiences prior to becoming a teacher. Think of volunteer experiences or jobs you were expected to perform to help your family. Be prepared to explain to students how those experiences helped you develop work habits that you use today.

ACTIVITY

1. Divide the class into small groups and distribute Work Study activity sheets to each student. Ask students in each group to name all the "jobs" they have had and write them on their activity sheets. Emphasize that the jobs do not have to be paid jobs, but might be regular duties they perform as a part of being in a family. Have them identify any jobs where they may have received some pay (yard work, babysitting, etc.).

2. Ask students to list all the job "skills" they developed from these jobs (e.g., physical stamina, child-care skills, high standards, etc.). [They may have some difficulty with this if they haven't thought about work skills before.]

3. Ask each group to develop a list of the 10 most common "jobs" and the skills associated with them. Have each group name occupations they might hold as adults that would require the same skills. Ask them to write these occupations on their activity sheets.

4. Ask each group to share with the rest of the class two common jobs (from their list) for students their age, skills they developed in those jobs, and where they might use those skills in future jobs.

DISCUSSION

1. What did you learn from this lesson?

2. How else will present jobs affect your future employment?

3. What makes a "good" worker?

 ## OPTIONAL ACTIVITY

Have students ask their parents or other family members about how they developed their work habits. Have them tell about all the household "jobs" for which they were responsible when growing up.

Adapted from Buchan and VanZandt. 1997. *Lessons for Life: A Complete Career Development Activities Library.* West Nyack, NY: The Center for Applied Research in Education.

WORK STUDY

JOBS I HAVE HAD

Job	Pay?	Skills

10 MOST COMMON JOBS FOR STUDENTS MY AGE

	Job	Skills
1.		
2.		
3.		
4.		
5.		
6.		
7.		
8.		
9.		
10.		

ADULT OCCUPATIONS REQUIRING SAME SKILLS:

SESSION 16:
TEAMWORK

OVERVIEW

This lesson will emphasize the importance of teamwork in creating a product that represents the interests of everyone in the group.

DURATION

Approximately 30 minutes

OBJECTIVES

1. Students will be able to express through symbols some aspect of their unique selves.

2. Students will be able to develop a product through cooperative teamwork.

3. Students will be able to describe how companies use teamwork to create better products.

MATERIALS

An array of discarded items or miscellaneous materials, such as scraps of yarn and cloth, paperclips, paper, buttons, bottle caps, small and thin pieces of wood, ribbon, and pictures from magazines. You may want to have students bring such things from home (nothing that is "needed," though!).

Glue and/or tape

PREPARATION

Think of how you will separate the materials so that everyone in the class has access to them while working in small groups.

ACTIVITY

1. Start the lesson by explaining that more and more successful companies in the global economy are looking for employees who are good team members. Teams are used to identify company needs, develop strategies for designing or improving products and services, and increasing revenue.

2. Create small groups of five or six students by having them count off according to the number of groups needed.

3. Using the materials you have gathered for this exercise, the students' task is to create a piece of artwork or model that represents or depicts at least one thing about each of the members in their group. Their product does not have to be functional, but they should try to create something that is aesthetically pleasing. Tell them the product should look better "as a whole" than as separate parts thrown together. (Give them about 15 minutes to create their product—a little longer if time allows.)

DISCUSSION

1. What are some of the challenges of working in teams?

2. What are some of the roles people played in the groups to accomplish the task?

3. Can people always "get their way" when working in a team?

4. What must happen with teams if they are to be productive?

5. Why would a team be better than having several people competing against each other in a company?

OPTIONAL ACTIVITY

Have each group choose a spokesperson who will describe the group's product and how it represents their "team."

SESSION 17:
WHAT'S THE DIFFERENCE?

OVERVIEW

Students will use their awareness of jobs in the vicinity of their homes as a point of reference in understanding the differences between an occupation and an industry.

DURATION

Approximately 30 minutes

OBJECTIVES

1. Students will be able to classify the kinds of industries that contribute to the local economy.

2. Students will be able to distinguish between jobs that are unique to an industry and those that are common in most industries.

MATERIALS

What's the Difference? activity sheet (copies for each student)

Industry Classification System (copies for each student)

PREPARATION

Look over the attached Industry Classification System. Use it as a reference. Students may come up with a different or better classification system. Your country may have a system for classifying industries. Call your Department of Labor (or a similar agency) for information.

ACTIVITY

1. Distribute What's the Difference? activity sheets and the Industry Classification System. Have students brainstorm all the jobs they can think of that exist in the local area and write the list on their activity sheets. Create a master list and put the list on the board.

2. Explain the difference between an occupation (a group of similar jobs found in different industries or organizations) and an industry (an establishment or group of establishments engaged in producing similar types of goods or services).

3. Ask students to create an industry classification system or use the one below. If you are not using the one below, write the system on the board.

4. In small groups, have students assign the jobs on the master list to specific industries.

5. Ask students to go over the remaining jobs to see if they seem to be related to occupation more than industry.

6. Ask students to identify what they consider to be the Top 5 Industries in their geographic area.

DISCUSSION

1. What is the difference between an occupation and an industry?

2. How do communities use information about industries?

3. What are the implications of pursuing a job that is industry-specific?

OPTIONAL ACTIVITY

Have students talk with a representative from the Department of Labor. Have them gather demographic information and possible projections about future industry growth.

ACTIVITY SHEET
WHAT'S THE DIFFERENCE?

Part 1:

1. List the jobs that exist in your local area.

JOBS IN MY LOCAL AREA

_____	_____
_____	_____
_____	_____
_____	_____
_____	_____
_____	_____
_____	_____
_____	_____
_____	_____
_____	_____

2. Copy the master list from the board on to your activity sheet.

MASTER LIST OF JOBS

_____	_____
_____	_____
_____	_____
_____	_____
_____	_____
_____	_____
_____	_____
_____	_____
_____	_____

Part 2:

There is a difference between an occupation and an industry.

An OCCUPATION is a group of similar jobs found in different industries or organizations.

An INDUSTRY is an establishment or group of establishments engaged in producing similar types of goods or services.

1. Using the industry classification system, write an industry in each box below.

2. Assign the jobs on the master list to specific industries.

INDUSTRY:	INDUSTRY:	INDUSTRY:	INDUSTRY:
JOBS:	JOBS:	JOBS:	JOBS:
1.	1.	1.	1.
2.	2.	2.	2.
3.	3.	3.	3.
4.	4.	4.	4.
5.	5.	5.	5.

INDUSTRY:	INDUSTRY:	INDUSTRY:	INDUSTRY:
JOBS:	JOBS:	JOBS:	JOBS:
1.	1.	1.	1.
2.	2.	2.	2.
3.	3.	3.	3.
4.	4.	4.	4.
5.	5.	5.	5.

INDUSTRY:	INDUSTRY:	INDUSTRY:	INDUSTRY:
JOBS:	JOBS:	JOBS:	JOBS:
1.	1.	1.	1.
2.	2.	2.	2.
3.	3.	3.	3.
4.	4.	4.	4.
5.	5.	5.	5.

Part 3:

List the Top Five Industries in your area.

FIVE TOP INDUSTRIES IN MY AREA

_____

_____

_____

_____

_____

INDUSTRY CLASSIFICATION SYSTEM

(Categories in which several workers are employed in a business or occupation with a common theme)

Agriculture

Communication

Construction

Entertainment

Financial Services

Fishing

Forestry

Health

Hospitality & Tourism (Recreation)

Information

Mining

Public Administration

Public Utilities (Telephone, Electricity, Water, etc.)

Real Estate

Retail Trade

Service

Transportation

Wholesale Trade

Miscellaneous

SESSION 18:
CHARTING THE REGION

OVERVIEW

Students will look at regions of the country and think about the effects of geographic settings on industries—and vice versa.

DURATION

Approximately 30 minutes

OBJECTIVES

1. Students will be able to identify the predominant industries in various regions of the country.

2. Students will be able to describe the effects of geographic settings and resources on industries and occupational choices.

3. Students will be able to describe the effects of industries on geographic regions within their country.

MATERIALS

Charting the Region activity sheet (copies for each student)

Map of the country with regions outlined or highlighted

PREPARATION

Have information available about such topics as natural resources, industries, attractions, physical geography, climate, cultural and political distinctions among the various regions of the country. Not every student needs this information, but it may be helpful for some to investigate these topics during the lesson.

ACTIVITY

1. Tell students that today's lesson is designed to help them look at the various industries in the country and to examine other factors that have an impact on local and regional economies.

2. Distribute Charting the Region activity sheets. Show students the map of the country and its regions. Have them identify the major industries of each region (e.g., mining, agriculture, government, tourism, etc.) on their activity sheets. (Use information resources if needed.)

3. Have students brainstorm a list of ways that the various industries have an impact on the people of the regions and write their suggestions on the activity sheets. Create and review a master list.

4. On another section of the board, have students brainstorm a list of ways that the regions have an impact on the industries and write their suggestions on the activity sheets. Create and review a master list.

DISCUSSION

1. What are the implications of the information we have listed on the board in terms of your future careers and occupational choices?

2. How might the picture change when we consider neighboring countries?

3. How are regional industries affected by the global economy?

4. What are some of the personal challenges you will face in examining your career options when you consider regional opportunities?

OPTIONAL ACTIVITY

Have students make a map that creatively depicts the lessons they have learned about regional industries and occupational opportunities.

CHARTING THE REGION

MAJOR INDUSTRIES IN MY COUNTRY'S REGIONS

REGION:	REGION:	REGION:	REGION:
INDUSTRY:	INDUSTRY:	INDUSTRY:	INDUSTRY:
1.	1.	1.	1.
2.	2.	2.	2.
3.	3.	3.	3.
4.	4.	4.	4.
5.	5.	5.	5.

REGION:	REGION:	REGION:	REGION:
INDUSTRY:	INDUSTRY:	INDUSTRY:	INDUSTRY:
1.	1.	1.	1.
2.	2.	2.	2.
3.	3.	3.	3.
4.	4.	4.	4.
5.	5.	5.	5.

HOW DO INDUSTRIES HAVE AN IMPACT ON THE PEOPLE?

HOW DO REGIONS HAVE AN IMPACT ON INDUSTRIES?

SESSION 19:
HERE'S HOW IT WORKS

OVERVIEW

This is a research project in which students investigate how the government keeps track of labor market information, job openings, national economic issues, etc.

DURATION

Two or three sessions of approximately 30 minutes each. Students may need a few days for research.

OBJECTIVES

1. Students will be able to apply research skills in identifying information about careers.

2. Students will be able to identify key information to use in conducting career searches.

MATERIALS

Here's How It Works research sheet (copies for each student)

Here's How It Works reference sheet (copies for each student)

PREPARATION

Do your own investigation prior to the lesson to identify key sources of career information. Identify agencies or resources (e.g., a daily newspaper) that students can contact to receive information about the labor market or other topics related to career development.

ACTIVITY

1. Explain to students that this lesson is designed to help them discover some of the resources they can use in understanding career opportunities.

2. Divide the class into four groups. Give each group one of the following topics to investigate:

    Labor Market Information

    Employment Trends & Projections

    Economic Concerns

    Job Openings

3. Distribute Here's How It Works research sheets. Have the groups create plans for investigating and reporting about the agencies and resources that are available on their topic. Their plans should include assignments for each member of their group.

4. Have students conduct their research outside class.

5. Distribute Here's How It Works reference sheets. Have the groups present their findings to the rest of the class. Tell them to identify the three resources they found most helpful for learning something about their topics. Tell the class to write the groups' recommendations on the reference sheets.

DISCUSSION

1. How can these resources be helpful in exploring career options?

2. What information was lacking that you will need when it comes time to make decisions about the occupation(s) you will pursue? How will you find that information?

3. What research skills did you apply to find the information you were seeking?

OPTIONAL ACTIVITIES

The reference sheet is a possible portfolio entry.

Each of the group topics is worthy of further discussion and exploration.

HERE'S HOW IT WORKS

TOPIC: _____

TO BE INVESTIGATED:

AGENCIES	RESOURCES

TASK ASSIGNMENTS

TASK	WHO WILL DO IT

HERE'S HOW IT WORKS

THREE MOST HELPFUL RESOURCES

LABOR MARKET INFORMATION

1.

2.

3.

EMPLOYMENT TRENDS & PROJECTIONS

1.

2.

3.

ECONOMIC CONCERNS

1.

2.

3.

JOB OPENINGS

1.

2.

3.

SESSION 20:
WHERE AM I GOING?

OVERVIEW

Students will use visual imagery to create a picture of the ideal life for themselves.

DURATION

Approximately 30 minutes

OBJECTIVES

1. Students will be able to describe what they perceive to be the ideal life for themselves in the future.

2. Students will be able to draw inferences from their ideal images about some of the priorities in their lives.

MATERIALS

Where Am I Going? activity sheet (copies for each student)

"Once Upon a Time in My Life" story

PREPARATION

None

ACTIVITY

1. Distribute Where Am I Going? activity sheets. Tell students today's lesson will be fun because it includes a story with a very interesting main character and the story has a happy ending. To participate, students need to close their eyes and use their imaginations to fill in the pictures and the details for the story you are going to narrate.

2. Read them the story "Once Upon a Time in My Life."

3. Have students open their eyes and write down what they imagined as the ideal family, the ideal place to live, and the ideal occupation, as well as their happy ending. Tell them to put their activity sheets into their portfolios.

DISCUSSION

1. Who is the main character in the story?
2. What do your ideal images suggest about what is important to you?
3. What gets in the way of people pursuing their ideal futures?
4. What do people need to do to keep focused on their ideal futures?

OPTIONAL ACTIVITY

Possible portfolio entry.

ONCE UPON A TIME IN MY LIFE

Once upon a time, there was a young person who was granted three wishes. However, unlike most wishes that give people lots of freedom about what they can wish for, this wish had several specific guidelines to follow. If the person altered the guidelines in any way (like trying to wish for one more thing!), all the wishes would disappear.

With closed eyes, the young person waited for the guidelines and the opportunity to fulfill the wishes. The first guideline was to imagine a time and place 15 years into the future. Let's see, that would make it the year _ _ _ _ [add 15 to the current year]. The first wish was to be able to have the ideal family. The young person thought for a few moments, then made the wish. Let your imagination tell you what this young person wished for as the ideal family. [Wait 15–20 seconds for the images to form.]

When the wish was complete, it was time to make the second wish, which was to name the ideal place to live. "You mean any place in the whole world?" the young person asked.

"Anywhere," was the reply.

What if I want to live in the same neighborhood where I live now?" the young person asked.

"Anywhere," was the reply.

So the young person wished for a place—the country, the town, the neighborhood, the kind of house—and it was fun thinking about the ideal place. Let your imagination tell you what the young person wished for. [Wait 20–30 seconds for the image to form.]

Finally, there was one more wish: To choose the perfect occupation. "You mean I have to work?" the young person asked. "Can't I just wish for no job at all?"

"It doesn't work that way," was the reply.

So the young person wished to be successfully employed in the ideal occupation. Let your imagination tell you what the young person wished for. [Wait 20–30 seconds.]

Now I know you were promised a happy ending to this story, so just imagine what that ending is. [Wait 20–30 seconds.]

WHERE AM I GOING?

MY IDEAL FAMILY:

MY IDEAL PLACE TO LIVE:

    Country:

    Town:

    Neighborhood:

    Kind of House:

MY IDEAL OCCUPATION:

MY HAPPY ENDING:

SESSION 21:
LAY THE FOUNDATION

OVERVIEW

Students will investigate the educational requirements for various occupations.

DURATION

Two sessions of approximately 30 minutes each

OBJECTIVE

Students will be able to identify the educational requirements for entering various occupations.

MATERIALS

Lay the Foundation activity sheet (copies for each student)

PREPARATION

1. Identify the federal or regional agency that oversees the credentialing (licensure, certification, etc.) of various occupations. Identify at least 10 occupations or professions that require credentialing that you can use as examples in class.

2. Ask a representative from an agency that oversees credentialing to visit the class and share information about credentialing and the importance of one's education for laying a foundation for career success.

  ## ACTIVITY

Day One

1. Explain that this lesson will focus on the education and technical training required to enter various professions.

2. Distribute copies of Lay the Foundation activity sheets. Ask students to think of occupations that probably require credentialing (e.g., electrician, nurse, teacher, accountant) and write them on the activity sheets. Write a master list on the board.

3. Using two occupations as examples, have students speculate about the coursework and supervised experiences that would be required for the proper credential. Keep a record of what the students listed as probable training requirements.

4. Explain that a guest speaker will be coming to the next class to talk about credentialing and to answer questions they have about educational and technical requirements for various occupations.

5. In small groups, have students generate a series of questions they can use for taking maximum advantage of the opportunity to learn about credentialing.

Homework

Encourage students to talk about the lesson on credentialing and to ask their parents if they have any questions they think students should be asking the guest speaker.

Day Two

Guest Speaker

DISCUSSION

As a follow-up to the guest speaker, ask:

1. What kind of an academic record will be needed to qualify for some of the training programs we have explored?

2. How can you use information from this lesson in exploring your career options?

3. Do some of the training programs require coursework that you were surprised about? Give some examples.

LAY THE FOUNDATION

OCCUPATIONS THAT REQUIRE CREDENTIALING

_____   _____

_____   _____

_____   _____

_____   _____

_____   _____

_____   _____

QUESTIONS FOR OUR EXPERT

1.

2.

3.

4.

5.

6.

7.

8.

9.

10.

SESSION 22:
POSITIVE DECISIONS

OVERVIEW

The lesson explores how one's self-concept influences decision-making.

DURATION

Approximately 30 minutes

OBJECTIVES

1. Students will be able to identify the difference between a positive and a negative self-concept.

2. Students will be able to describe how one's self-concept influences decision-making.

MATERIALS

Positive Decisions Role-Plays (copies for each role player)

PREPARATION

1. Prepare copies of the role-playing situations for the two people who will be doing the role-plays.

2. Write the terms *positive self-concept* and *negative self-concept* at the top of two different sections of the board.

ACTIVITY

1. Ask students: What is a positive self-concept? What is a negative self-concept? How does a person with a positive self-concept act? How does a person with a negative self-concept act?

2. Ask for two student volunteers to do some role-playing (or have three sets of two volunteers each).

3. Tell student volunteers that you will be giving them some role-playing situations that they are to act out, and distribute Positive Decisions Role-Plays. They can choose whether they want to use positive or negative self-concept traits first. But they will be acting out each scenario by demonstrating behavior that is positive in one and negative in the other. The rest of the class will analyze the performance and determine whether the decision maker is operating from a positive or negative self-concept.

4. Have students act out the scenarios for two to three minutes.

5. Ask the rest of the class to suggest other behaviors that might also emerge in these situations if the person were behaving from a different self-concept.

DISCUSSION

1. What did you like about this lesson?

2. What did you learn about self-concept and its effect on decision-making?

3. How can this lesson be applied to what we are learning about career development?

POSITIVE DECISIONS ROLE-PLAYS

Role-Playing Situations

- You have two days off from school because the teachers are attending a special workshop. You're trying to figure out what to do with your spare time.

- You're feeling pretty stressed out lately because you have so much to do. How do you deal with it all?

- You need to make a decision about entering a sports training program. How do you decide?

SESSION 23:
CREATING OPPORTUNITIES

OVERVIEW

Students will work in groups to generate ideas for an imaginary business that will help them explore the concept of entrepreneurship.

DURATION

Two or three sessions of approximately 30 minutes each (depending on how thoroughly you want to explore the concept and how much fun students are having with the activity)

OBJECTIVES

1. Students will be able to identify the necessary variables for becoming an entrepreneur.

2. Students will be able to create an entrepreneurial approach to addressing a local need.

MATERIALS

Creating Opportunities activity sheet (copies for each student)

PREPARATION

Check with government or private agencies to see if there is information available about becoming an entrepreneur.

ACTIVITY

1. Ask students if they have ever heard of an entrepreneur. Explain that it is a term that comes from the French word *entreprendre* which means "to undertake." The definition of entrepreneur is "one who organizes, manages, and assumes the risk of a business or enterprise." In today's global economy, people who are entrepreneurs find opportunities related to the changing world of work. They are individuals who recognize that they need or want to be in charge of their own futures and they will create situations whereby opportunities come their way.

2. To identify "opportunities related to change," have students create a list of all the businesses or services they would like to see in their town that do not already exist.

3. Form the class into small groups and distribute copies of Creating Opportunities activity sheets. Have each group form a business team and choose one item from the "opportunity list" (of businesses or services) to be the focus of their new business.

4. Once the groups have chosen their enterprise, have them generate a list of all the things that must be considered and all the things that must be in place for the entrepreneurial enterprise to be a success.

5. Have them assign responsibilities for various facets of the enterprise and provide job titles that represent the responsibilities.

DISCUSSION

1. How difficult or easy is it to be an entrepreneur?

2. What do you think the typical challenges are for entrepreneurs?

3. What personal characteristics would seem to be most helpful for a person wanting to be an entrepreneur?

4. What are some things students should start thinking about now if they want to become entrepreneurs?

OPTIONAL ACTIVITY

Have students carry out their plans for a local enterprise through a mock-business venture.

CREATING OPORTUNITIES

OUR NEW BUSINESS IS:

WHAT WE MUST CONSIDER TO MAKE IT A SUCCESS:

1.

2.

3.

4.

5.

6.

7.

8.

9.

10.

BUSINESS RESPONSIBILITIES:

NAME:_____

FUNCTION:_____ TITLE:_____

NAME:_____

FUNCTION:_____ TITLE:_____

NAME:_____

FUNCTION:_____ TITLE:_____

NAME:_____

FUNCTION:_____ TITLE:_____

NAME:_____

FUNCTION:_____ TITLE:_____

SESSION 24:
HOW I SEE THINGS

OVERVIEW

Students will create a drawing that depicts their possible career options.

DURATION

Approximately 30 minutes

OBJECTIVES

1. Students will be able to identify possible career options for further exploration.

2. Students will be able to creatively represent the connections among their career options.

MATERIALS

Colored pencils, markers, paints, or crayons
Drawing paper

PREPARATION

Gather art supplies or remind students to bring them for the lesson.

ACTIVITY

1. Take about five minutes to review the previous lessons in this unit. Tell the students to think about how they have used the lessons to narrow their choices of possible occupations to pursue.

2. Tell students to identify five or six occupations that they find fascinating and about which they would like to have more information.

3. For the rest of the class, have students create drawings that represent the choices they are considering and the way they feel about the process of making a tentative career decision. Allow them the opportunity to use whatever medium they prefer as well as the artistic style with which they feel most comfortable (from stick drawings to abstract).

4. Display the drawings in the room (for just the day or for a longer "showing" so others outside the classroom can see their work).

DISCUSSION

1. As you look around the room at the various drawings, what messages seem to surface about how students feel about their career options?

2. How did it feel to visually connect your options and your exploration process?

3. What did you enjoy about this activity?

4. What did you find challenging about the activity?

OPTIONAL ACTIVITY

As a more advanced art experience, invite parents for a reception and art show. Have students prepare the drinks and snacks for the reception and then be available to explain their drawing to others.

Unit Two:
Competency Checklist

As a result of my participation in Unit Two, I ... (Check those items for which you feel you have attained competency.)

- [ ] ... appreciate the traits and skills I must possess to do a thorough job of investigating my career options.

- [ ] ... am aware of the challenges I face as I explore my career options.

- [ ] ... have a sense of the major life roles that contribute to career satisfaction.

- [ ] ... appreciate the fact that I am responsible for creating my own sense of balance among the various life roles.

- [ ] ... can name some of the work habits I have developed that will help me when I am employed.

- [ ] ... know some of the personal strengths and traits I possess that can contribute to a group project.

- [ ] ... appreciate how teamwork is used in work situations.

- [ ] ... can distinguish between jobs that are unique to an industry and jobs that are common to most industries.

- [ ] ... am aware of some of the major industries in my region of the country.

- [ ] ... know several sources of information I can use for investigating occupations.

- [ ] ... know the kind of life I would like to have in the future if there were no obstacles.

- [ ] ... know whether particular credentials are needed for the different career options I am exploring.

- [ ] ... recognize how my self-concept can influence the way I make decisions.

- [ ] ... appreciate some of the challenges of starting a new business and being an entrepreneur.

- [ ] ... know how I feel right now about my future career options.

• UNIT THREE: CAREER-PLANNING
How Do I Get There?

UNIT THREE: CAREER-PLANNING
HOW DO I GET THERE?

If you intend to take a trip to a location where you've never been before, it's probably a good idea to take along a map. Of course, some people like an adventure, but most people would find it a bit unnerving to head into territory where risks are involved and the unknown lurks in the shadows. One's career journey can seem just that threatening at times when the possibilities present so many "unknowns." That's why career-planning is important. It gives the individual a sense of direction, anticipates some of the dangers, and provides some reassurance about being on the right path.

Students in the middle grades are already dealing with the unsettling realities of their physical and emotional changes. Career decision-making shouldn't add another layer to the stress. To the contrary, career-planning strategies might provide the one sense of stability they need for helping to shape the identity they are so diligently seeking. If the foundation for career awareness and exploration has been sufficient, the career-planning process should come as a sense of relief as adolescents head into their high-school years with some goals in mind.

The transition from the middle grades to the high-school level marks another developmental milestone in students' lives. The career-planning process can help to create a smoother transition as students anticipate some of the changes that will take place during their high-school years and develop strategies for maximizing the experience.

The career-planning process in the middle grades is slightly different from the more definitive planning process students will experience during high school. But it is no less important. In fact, it may be more important, since the planning done in the middle grades can be a primary factor in determining how seriously students tackle their high-school studies and take advantage of the opportunities that are available to them in their communities. The planning that is done in the middle-school years is referred to as tentative planning, since it is recognized that adolescence is a time when students tend to vacillate in their needs and priorities. A primary goal of the planning process in the middle grades is to get students to anticipate some of the plausibilities and possibilities in their future. And to make tentative plans that will enhance that future.

The lessons in this unit focus on promoting an understanding of a planning process, helping students develop a long-range perspective for planning, and developing the skills to nurture their entry into, and success in, a challenging job market. The first lesson introduces students to the idea of keeping a portfolio. And the succeeding lessons provide several opportunities for them to make entries into the portfolio that represent their best thinking and best work. One lesson, in particular, asks students to seek "words of wisdom" in planning their futures. As the instructor for this curriculum, you have an opportunity to add your own words of wisdom to each of the lessons and to model the process of using the awareness, exploration, and planning sequence as a foundation for lifelong learning.

SESSION 25:
MY BEST WORK

OVERVIEW

Students will be introduced to the use of portfolios for monitoring their career development, emphasizing that portfolios should contain their best work.

DURATION

Approximately 30 minutes

OBJECTIVES

1. Students will be able to explain how portfolios are used to store and retrieve important information about themselves as an integral part of understanding their career development.

2. Students will be able to develop criteria for determining their best work.

3. Students will be able to choose examples of their best work for entry in their portfolios.

MATERIALS

Art supplies
Colored file folders

PREPARATION

Although it is not essential, it might be fun for you to prepare a folder that you will call your Professional Portfolio. Think about the titles you will give to the sections of the portfolio.

ACTIVITY

1. Ask students if they have ever heard of an artist's portfolio. What is it for? How do artists decide what goes into the portfolio?

2. Tell them they are going to make folders today that they will use to store information that they want to save from the career development curriculum.

3. Explain that one of the key concepts they should learn about portfolios is that the items that are stored inside should represent their best work. Write the words BEST WORK on the board. What does it mean? Who decides what constitutes one's best work? Have students brainstorm and refine the criteria that might be considered for assessing one's best work in a career portfolio.

4. Have students select the criteria from the brainstormed list that they will use for choosing items to go into their career portfolios.

5. Distribute the file folders and art supplies. Have students create a cover for their portfolios that represents their criteria for best work. The cover should include the name of the student under the title *Exploring Future Options*.

Exploring Future Options

Jane Smith

DISCUSSION

1. How can portfolios help you understand and enhance your career development?

2. What are some of the challenges you anticipate as you start work on your portfolio?

3. Who are the people who will see the contents of your portfolio? How can the portfolio highlight the things that matter most to you?

SESSION 26:
PLAN YOUR PLAN

OVERVIEW

Students will investigate how others plan for significant events or for accomplishing tasks and borrow ideas to shape their own method of planning.

DURATION

Two sessions of approximately 30 minutes each

OBJECTIVES

1. Students will be able to recognize differential means of planning.
2. Students will be able to synthesize what they have learned about planning strategies to create their own model of planning.

MATERIALS

Plan Your Plan activity sheets (copies for each student)

PREPARATION

Think about your own method of planning for major events or tasks. Be prepared to explain it in case students ask.

ACTIVITY

Day One

1. Ask students to name the kinds of events or tasks that usually require considerable planning (e.g., holiday events, sports competition, building a house, making a quilt). Write their responses on the board.

2. Ask whether each kind of task or event requires the same kind of planning. Why or why not? Have students describe some of the differences.

3. Distribute copies of Plan Your Plan activity sheets and explain the homework assignment. Have students interview two different people, asking the individuals to explain their process for planning important events or accomplishing significant tasks. Have them list the steps.

Ask students to put a checkmark next to the planning strategies that appear in both planning models.

Day Two

1. In class, have students meet in small groups and share the various methods of planning.
2. Give students five to ten minutes to reflect on what they have heard and to use the information to create a generic planning model for themselves that incorporates all the best ideas from the sharing.

DISCUSSION

What are the most important lessons you have learned about planning?

PLAN YOUR PLAN

Part 1:

1. Interview two people and have them explain their process for planning important events (for example, your grandparent who always hosts the holiday gathering) or for accomplishing a significant task (a coach trying to win a soccer match against a traditional rival). Ask them to list the steps they take.

2. Put a checkmark next to the planning strategies that appear in both planning models.

Name: #1:_____

Steps in Planning:

1.

2.

3.

4.

5.

6.

7.

8.

9.

10.

Name: #2:_____

Steps in Planning:

1.

2.

3.

4.

5.

6.

7.

8.

9.

10.

Part 2:

List the steps in your personal planning model.

STEPS IN MY PERSONAL PLANNING MODEL

1.

2.

3.

4.

5.

6.

7.

8.

9.

10.

WINDOW SHOPPING

OVERVIEW

Students will explore educational requirements and opportunities for pursuing their career aspirations.

DURATION

Two sessions of approximately 30 minutes each

OBJECTIVES

1. Students will be able to identify the general training requirements for pursuing careers in various occupations.

2. Students will be able to summarize tentative educational goals related to their career aspirations.

MATERIALS

Window shopping activity sheet (copies for each student)
Index cards
Masking tape
Information about high-school-level vocational training programs, academies, and academic programs, as well as programs offered in the local high-school(s), if available.
Any brochure or pamphlets about post-secondary vocational schools and universities would also be helpful.

PREPARATION

 none

ACTIVITY

Day One

1. Ask students to describe the practice of "window shopping" (i.e., looking but not necessarily buying). Explain that one of the important parts of career-planning is a lot like window shopping. Before they commit to a plan, they should check out their options. Today's lesson focuses on their educational options. Distribute Window Shopping activity sheets.

2. Have students individually list four or five possible occupational choices to which they are giving careful consideration.

3. In small groups, have students create lists of local programs and academies that train people for the professions that the group members are considering. Have them discuss what they have heard about the various programs and schools and summarize their findings on the activity sheets.

Homework

Discuss the homework assignment. Tell students to add to their informal list of educational institutions by asking others at home or in their neighborhoods about programs they have heard about. Also, ask them to inquire about local post-secondary vocational schools and universities.

Day Two

1. Assemble the students in their original groups. Have the students collate the information they have gathered on index cards. Have each group present its information to the entire class.

2. Have the students post their index cards on a wall with masking tape. (If they have information about both high school-level programs and post-secondary institutions, post the names on separate boards.)

DISCUSSION

1. Why is it a good idea to do some window shopping about educational programs at such a young age?

2. How is listening to others' information and opinions about the various educational programs like window shopping?

3. How rigorous are some of these programs?

4. What have you learned about the educational decisions that lie ahead for you?

WINDOW SHOPPING

Part 1:

Instructions:
List four or five occupations you are considering.

OCCUPATIONS I AM CONSIDERING:

1.

2.

3.

4.

5.

Part 2:

Instructions:
List local programs or schools that train people for these professions.

TRAINING PROGRAM: _____

Occupations for Which It Offers Training:

1.

2.

3.

4.

5.

Description: _____

_____

_____

TRAINING PROGRAM: _____

Occupations for Which It Offers Training:

1.

2.

3.

4.

5.

Description: _____
_____
_____

TRAINING PROGRAM: _____

Occupations for Which It Offers Training:

1.

2.

3.

4.

5.

Description: _____
_____
_____

TRAINING PROGRAM: _____

Occupations for Which It Offers Training:

1.

2.

3.

4.

5.

Description: _____
_____
_____

MAKING WISE CHOICES

OVERVIEW

Students will interview workers from different age brackets and collect "words of wisdom" about planning for a career.

DURATION

Two sessions of approximately 30 minutes each

OBJECTIVE

Students will be able to analyze information they have collected about career-planning and draw conclusions that are pertinent for their own personal planning.

MATERIALS

Making Wise Choices activity sheet (copies for each student)

PREPARATION

None

  ## ACTIVITY

Day One

1. Explain that this lesson uses the wisdom of others to shape our own wisdom.

2. Divide the class into small groups and distribute Making Wise Choices activity sheets. Tell the students that they are to create an outline for conducting brief interviews with individuals about what they have learned from their work experiences and advice they would give about career-planning. Have the students write the outline on the activity sheet.

Homework

As a homework assignment, they are each to interview four different workers. Each worker should be from a different decade in terms of age.

Day Two

1. Have each member of the class share their favorite piece of wisdom. Encourage students to write down the ones that they would like to remember.

2. Give the students 10–15 minutes to create a page for their portfolios on which they record the most important words of wisdom they want to use as they plan their careers. Encourage them to create pages that are aesthetically pleasing and that represent their best work.

DISCUSSION

1. What did you enjoy most about this lesson?

2. Were there certain themes that seemed to come through in the words of wisdom being offered by experienced workers?

3. Did the age of the workers make any difference in the kinds of messages people had to offer?

OPTIONAL ACTIVITY

Create a compendium of the messages students collected and send copies home to parents.

MAKING WISE CHOICES

Part 1:

Instructions:
Create an outline for conducting brief interviews with individuals about what they have learned from their work experiences and advice they would give about career-planning. Write the outline below.

INTERVIEW OUTLINE:

Part 2:

Instructions:
Interview four different workers, each from a different decade in terms of age, about what they have learned from their work experiences and advice they would give about career-planning. Write their "words of wisdom" below.

Name:_____

"Words of Wisdom":_____
_____
_____
_____

Name:_____

"Words of Wisdom":_____
_____
_____
_____

Name:_____

"Words of Wisdom":_____
_____
_____
_____

Name:_____

"Words of Wisdom":_____
_____
_____
_____

TAKE THE STAGE

OVERVIEW

Students will assess their progress in the Awareness-Exploration-Planning process of career development.

DURATION

Approximately 30 minutes

OBJECTIVES

1. Students will be able to describe the stages of the career development process.

2. Students will be able to recognize stages of career development from evidence of individual behavior.

MATERIALS

Take the Stage activity sheet (copies for each student)

PREPARATION

Write Awareness ▶ Exploration ▶ Preparation on the board

ACTIVITY

1. Remind students that this curriculum is based on the Awareness ▶ Exploration ▶ Preparation model of career development. The self-knowledge (or "Who Am I?") lessons have been about awareness, as have been some of the lessons about the "World of Work." The "Where Am I Going?" unit was about career exploration and planning and encouraged them to start thinking about tentative choices. The career preparation unit is focusing on career-planning.

2. Ask students to choose action verbs that describe how people would typically act in the various stages of this model (e.g., observe, investigate, train, etc.).

3. Distribute Take the Stage activity sheets, review, and ask students to complete them. Once students have finished the assignment, discuss their findings. The appropriate answers are listed below:

- a person doing library research about a particular occupation (could be either awareness or exploration, depending on how the person uses the information);
- a person "shadowing" another person on the job to see if the work is as exciting as it sounded in the book (exploration);
- a worker who has been in the same job for eight years, but doesn't really like her job and wishes she could do something else (awareness);
- a fifth-grade student who asks a teacher for a letter of recommendation to attend a summer science camp (preparation);
- a skilled worker who experiences a handicapping injury and can no longer work in his chosen field (awareness).

DISCUSSION

1. Is there complete agreement about the classification of the examples?

2. How might a person's awareness of this sequential process help in determining the next steps to take in the career-planning process?

3. What else do you need to know to take full advantage of the preparation stage for your own career development, especially when you think about planning for and entering the high-school level?

TAKE THE STAGE

The three stages of career development are:

AWARENESS ▸ EXPLORATION ▸ PREPARATION

Instructions:
Below are examples of people's behavior. Name the stage at which the individual is probably functioning in the career development process:

- a person doing library research about a particular occupation

  Stage: _____

- a person "shadowing" another person on the job to see if the work is as exciting as it sounded in the book

  Stage: _____

- a worker who has been in the same job for 8 years, but doesn't really like her job and wishes she could do something else

  Stage: _____

- a fifth-grade student who asks a teacher for a letter of recommendation to attend a summer science camp

  Stage: _____

- a skilled worker who experiences a handicapping injury and can no longer work in his chosen field

  Stage: _____

SESSION 30:
BEST FOOT FORWARD

OVERVIEW

This lesson provides an opportunity for students to role-play interview situations where they have to demonstrate interpersonal skills that are valued in many work situations.

DURATION

Approximately 30–45 minutes

OBJECTIVES

1. Students will be able to identify typical interpersonal skills that are valued in the workplace.

2. Students will be able to demonstrate effective interpersonal skills in a mock-interview situation.

MATERIALS

None

PREPARATION

None

ACTIVITY

1. Explain that today's lesson focuses on some of the personal skills needed to be successful in most occupations. Because these skills are used in interactions between and among other people, they are referred to as interpersonal skills. Note that some studies have shown that as many people are fired from their jobs because of poor interpersonal skills as for incompetence (lack of technical job skills).

2. Ask students to brainstorm a list of the kinds of interpersonal skills and traits that would be beneficial for jobs that require interactions with the public. List the skills and traits on the board.

3. Ask the students to identify the three or four interpersonal skills that are most important for a worker to demonstrate. Try to reach consensus.

4. In groups of four (one potential employee, one employer, two observers), have the students role-play a job interview situation where the interviewee is applying for an entry-level job. All the people being interviewed have the necessary qualifications, so the candidate needs to convince the employer that they are the best among all the qualified people being interviewed. Tell observers what to look for. (Allow 5–10 minutes for the interview.)

5. Have the observers discuss what they noticed in the interview and which interpersonal skills seemed to work most effectively for the job candidate.

DISCUSSION

1. Why should middle-school students be practicing job interviews?

2. Can interpersonal skills be "turned on" for an interview, and then be very different in reality?

3. How can employers distinguish between the genuine people and the ones who are phony?

4. What did you learn from this lesson that you can use in your career preparation?

Adapted from Buchan and VanZandt. 1997. *Lessons for Life: A Complete Career Development Activities Library.* West Nyack, NY: The Center for Applied Research in Education.

SESSION 31:
LIFELONG COMMITMENTS

OVERVIEW

This lesson explores the concept of lifelong learning. Students interview people who have been in the workforce for at least 10 years to discover what kind of continuing education has been required for them to remain current in their jobs.

DURATION

Two sessions of approximately 30 minutes each

OBJECTIVES

1. Students will be able to explain the concept of lifelong learning.

2. Students will be able to draw inferences about their future responsibilities as lifelong learners from interviews with established workers.

MATERIALS

Lifelong Commitments activity sheet (copies for each student)

PREPARATION

None

ACTIVITY

Day One

1. Explain the concept of lifelong learning. (The demands of an ever-changing world require that we continue to learn new knowledge and skills for the rest of our lives if we are to remain competitive in the job market. At the highest level of learning, people "learn for the sake of learning.")

2. Distribute Lifelong Commitments activity sheets and explain the homework assignment. They are to interview a person who has been in the same occupation for at least 10 years to investigate the concept of lifelong learning.

3. Arrange students in small groups. Have them discuss the kinds of questions that should be used to interview the workers.

4. Have them finalize their list of questions before they conduct their interview.

Day Two

Have students report what they discovered.

DISCUSSION

1. What did you learn about lifelong learning from hearing all the reports about experienced workers?

2. How does lifelong learning work?

3. After you finish your formal schooling, what kinds of lifelong learning do you see for yourselves?

LIFELONG COMMITMENTS

In this assignment, you will interview someone who has been in the same occupation for at least 10 years to investigate lifelong learning.

PART 1:

Instructions:

Below, list the questions you will ask during the interview.

INTERVIEW QUESTIONS:

1.

2.

3.

4.

5.

PART 2:

Instructions:

Below, write a summary of your interview.

INTERVIEW SUMMARY:

SESSION 32:
BENCHMARKS

OVERVIEW

Students will use the concept of benchmarks to determine the kinds of criteria they will use for measuring their progress in their career development.

DURATION

Approximately 30 minutes

OBJECTIVE

Students will be able to identify the criteria they will use for measuring their progress and success in their careers.

MATERIALS

Benchmark activity sheet (copies for each student)

PREPARATION

None

ACTIVITY

1. Ask students if they have heard of benchmarks. The dictionary definition is "a point of reference from which a measurement may be made."

2. Have the students brainstorm all the milestones in one's career when a "measurement" a) should be taken as a way of determining whether appropriate progress is being made or b) could be taken to document their success. Make sure they are not limited by seeing measurement as "passing a test." Remind them that their career is their life, not just their occupation. Record their ideas on the board.

3. Distribute Benchmarks activity sheets. Using the brainstormed ideas from the board as a point of reference, have the students make a list of the benchmarks that will define their progress and success in life. Recommend that they include their work in their portfolio.

DISCUSSION

1. How will these benchmarks serve you in your career development?

2. Are your standards high enough? Are they too high?

3. What happens if you do not live up to the criteria you have set for yourself?

4. How will family members and employers view your benchmarks of success?

5. How seriously should you take these benchmarks?

OPTIONAL ACTIVITY

Have students complete a life-line exercise and include their benchmarks of progress or success on the life-line.

BENCHMARKS

BENCHMARKS THAT WILL DEFINE PROGRESS AND SUCCESS IN MY LIFE

1.

2.

3.

4.

5.

6.

7.

8.

9.

10.

SESSION 33:
FIRST IMPRESSIONS

OVERVIEW

Students will use their anonymous observations of people in the workforce to assess how communication skills contribute to positive or negative first impressions.

DURATION

Two sessions of approximately 30 minutes each

OBJECTIVES

1. Students will be able to explain how one's communication skills can create strong first impressions.

2. Students will be able to generalize what they have learned about first impressions and make conscious decisions about what they will do to monitor how their communication skills might make an impression on others.

MATERIALS

First Impressions activity sheet (copies for each student)

PREPARATION

None

  ## ACTIVITY

Day One:

1. Explain that this lesson will focus on what makes a good—or a bad—first impression. There are many kinds of behaviors and traits that contribute to an individual's first impression, but this lesson will only focus on communication skills.

2. Distribute First Impressions activity sheets. In small groups, have the students identify what they consider to be the top five communication skills that contribute to a positive first impression (e.g., good eye contact, follows directions accurately) and the top five com-

munication skills that contribute to a negative first impression (e.g., poor grammar and/or spelling; monopolizing a conversation). Make sure everyone writes down their Top Five lists on the activity sheet.

Homework

Tell students that you want them to become more conscious of how people are influenced by communication skills. They are to anonymously (excluding friends and family members) observe people on the street, in stores, in the park, on the telephone, etc. They should note when they have a strong reaction to an individual; observe from afar, but try to focus on the person's communication skills. Using their Top Five lists from class, they should try to determine whether the person's communications skills were contributing to their first impression. They should note their reactions on a sheet of paper, but make no contact with the individual. Emphasize that the point of the assignment is not to critique the person, but to become conscious of how first impressions are made.

Day Two:

1. In class, have students share what they learned about communication skills, without mentioning who they observed or where they observed them.

2. As a final reflection, have the students personalize this lesson by noting what they are going to monitor about their own communication skills as a result of what they observed and heard. Tell them to put this in their portfolios.

DISCUSSION

1. What was most challenging about this lesson?

2. How easy is it to be aware of the impressions we make on others?

3. What is the importance of first impressions when you enter the world of work?

4. How is the concept of first impressions connected to career-planning?

5. What are the implications for individual action?

OPTIONAL ACTIVITY

If the observation exercise seems too invasive, have the students conduct a role-playing exercise in which some individuals consciously try to use certain positive or negative communication skills to project a certain impression. Then ask those who were observing to give their reactions. Check for agreement between intended impressions and those that were observed.

FIRST IMPRESSIONS

TOP FIVE

PART 1:

Instructions:

Identify the top five communication skills that contribute to a positive and negative first impression.

FIVE COMMUNICATION SKILLS THAT CONTRIBUTE TO A POSITIVE FIRST IMPRESSION:

1.

2.

3.

4.

5.

FIVE COMMUNICATION SKILLS THAT CONTRIBUTE TO A NEGATIVE FIRST IMPRESSION:

1.

2.

3.

4.

5.

PART 2:

Instructions:

Note what you are going to monitor about your own communication skills as a result of what you observed and heard.

WHAT I WILL MONITOR ABOUT MY COMMUNICATIONS SKILLS

1.

2.

3.

4.

5.

SESSION 34:
POWER OF THE STARS

OVERVIEW

Using television characters as a reference, students will analyze how positive and negative work habits contribute to a person's credibility.

DURATION

Approximately 30 minutes

OBJECTIVES

1. Students will be able to identify positive and negative work habits exhibited by fictitious characters.

2. Students will be able to describe how good skills and positive work habits contribute to one's credibility.

MATERIALS

Power of the Stars activity sheet (copies for each student)

PREPARATION

None

ACTIVITY

1. Distribute Power of the Stars activity sheets. Have the students record the names of ten famous television characters with prominent roles who demonstrate positive job skills. They can range from actors to news reporters to cartoon characters.

2. Tell students to review their lists and for each character ask, "What are some of this person's positive job skills?" List three skills for each character.

3. Divide students into small groups and have them place the characters in rank order, with the person who has the strongest job skills ranked #1. Then have them choose a final group of five characters they would hire to be on their work team if they were to have such an opportunity. Ask them to try to come to a consensus.

4. Have the spokesperson from each group name their choices and summarize why these were the best. Ask the students to note the differences and similarities of the lists.

5. Ask "Does this mean that these individuals have more credibility than everyone else?"

DISCUSSION

1. Which job skills seemed to be the most positive ones these workers possessed?

2. Are these the kinds of worker traits and skills that always make individuals stand out as "better than the rest"?

3. How can students in middle school exhibit these work habits?

4. How do good skills and work habits contribute to one's credibility? What else contributes to a person's credibility?

Adapted from Buchan and VanZandt. 1997. *Lessons for Life: A Complete Career Development Activities Library.* West Nyack, NY: The Center for Applied Research in Education.

POWER OF THE STARS

Instructions:

1. Record the names of 10 famous television characters with prominent roles who demonstrate positive job skills.

2. List three specific positive job skills for each.

10 FAMOUS TELEVISION CHARACTERS WHO DEMONSTRATE POSITIVE JOB SKILLS

Name:_____

Skills:

1.

2.

3.

Name:_____

Skills:

1.

2.

3.

Name:_____

Skills:

1.

2.

3.

Name:_____

Skills:

1.

2.

3.

Name:_____

Skills:

1.

2.

3.

Name:_____

Skills:

1.

2.

3.

Name:_____

Skills:

1.

2.

3.

Name:_____

Skills:

1.

2.

3.

Name:_____

Skills:

1.

2.

3.

Name:_____

Skills:

1.

2.

3.

SESSION 35:
CREATING A NETWORK

OVERVIEW

The lesson focuses on the importance of building a network to assist with creating career opportunities and for support throughout one's career.

DURATION

Approximately 30 minutes

OBJECTIVES

1. Students will be able to describe why a support network is helpful during career-planning.

2. Students will be able to generate lists of people and resources that will serve as their support networks as they participate in various activities related to career-planning, career placement, and career success.

MATERIALS

Creating a Network activity sheet (copies for each student)

PREPARATION

You may want to write down the names of people, agencies, associations, and other resources that you consider integral parts of your support network. Be prepared to share examples of how your network has assisted you during different phases of your career.

   ## ACTIVITY

1. Use a spider web as a visual metaphor to explain the concept of career networking: The webs are often very difficult to see, but they still provide the critical support the spider needs for survival. The strength of the web is more important than the size. Feel free to offer other examples.

2. Distribute Creating a Network activity sheets. Ask students to think of individuals who they are confident will always be there to offer support or suggestions when they enter different phases of their career-planning process. Ask them to write their names at each point of the web. They should be as specific as possible.

3. Have students share some of the kinds of people they are including in their support network. (At this level of sharing, general categories like "my uncle" will be more helpful to those still looking for ideas than the specifics such as William Budd.)

4. Have students select adjectives that describe the individuals who were included on the support webs. Record the adjectives on the board.

DISCUSSION

1. Why is it wise to have a support network when involved in career-planning?

2. What do you expect from the people in your support network?

3. Should people always rely on their own competence to create career opportunities for them or should they use their support network for finding out about names and resources?

4. How does your support network fit in with your plans for a successful future?

ALTERNATIVE ACTIVITY

Have students share their networks with their families and see if they have more suggestions for strengthening the network.

CREATING A NETWORK

SESSION 36:
OPENING DOORS TO MY FUTURE

OVERVIEW

Students will use an education plan to think about how their high-school years can help them plan for future career success.

DURATION

Several sessions of approximately 30 minutes each

OBJECTIVES

1. Students will be able to identify, reflect upon, and synthesize information they have learned about themselves.

2. Students will be able to choose tentative career goals based on their career awareness, exploration, and planning process.

3. Students will be able to develop tentative educational plans to address their career goals.

MATERIALS

Education Planner (copies for each student)
Certificates

PREPARATION

- Make sure you have enough Education Planners for each student—or develop a strategy for having students create their own Education Planners

- Peruse the Education Planner

- Decide how many class sessions will be needed for students to complete their Education Planners

 ## ACTIVITY

1. Explain to students that the last few sessions of the career-development curriculum will be devoted to drawing together much of the information from the Awareness (Self-knowledge), Exploration, and Planning units and using that information to complete an Education Planner that helps them think about their transition to high school.

2. Pass out the Education Planners (or have students create their own planners).

3. Have the students fill in the personal information section.

4. On a separate sheet of paper (NOT their Education Planner), have students jot down some ideas about the kind of information they would like to include in the self-knowledge section. After about 10 minutes of reflecting and writing, put the students in small groups of four to five students and have them share their tentative responses to the self-knowledge section. When they are done sharing, tell them to take the information home with them, reflect some more, revise and refine their responses, and create messages that reflect their "best work."

5. Repeat the process as necessary until students finish their Education Planner.

6. Award students certificates of completion and tell them that they can take their portfolios home and use them in the future to plan their career moves.

DISCUSSION

1. How easy or difficult has it been to complete this education plan?

2. How do you think the Education Planner will help you as you enter high school?

OPTIONAL ACTIVITY

Develop a special celebration where students can share their education plans and receive validation for their reflection and direction.

Education Planner

PERSONAL INFORMATION

Name: _____

Address: _____

Phone: _____ Date: _____

School: _____

Teacher: _____

SELF-KNOWLEDGE

The important things I need to remember about myself as I plan my education are the following:

1.

2.

3.

4.

5.

EXPLORATION

MY LIKES AND DISLIKES

I have discovered some of my likes and dislikes about career options as follows:

1.

2.

3.

4.

5.

CAREER OPTIONS THAT INTEREST ME

I would like to explore the following career options:

1.

2.

3.

4.

5.

KEY FACTORS

The key factors in this decision are (interest, abilities, work values, lifestyle, earning potential, strengths, personal realities):

1.

2.

3.

4.

5.

PLANNING

EDUCATIONAL OBJECTIVES

Based on what I have learned about myself and my tentative career options, my educational objectives in high school will be:

1.

2.

3.

4.

5.

STEPS TO TAKE

I will take the following steps to achieve my educational objectives:

1.

2.

3.

4.

5.

has successfully completed the

Career Development Curriculum

Exploring Future Options

_____
Teacher's Name

_____
School

_____
Date

Unit Three:
Competency Checklist

As a result of my participation in Unit Three, I ... (Check those items for which you feel you have attained competency.)

- [ ] ... appreciate how my career portfolio can help me collect and use my best thinking and best work for making career choices.

- [ ] ... have developed my own criteria for determining what I think is my best work.

- [ ] ... have collected several examples of my best work to help me with my career-planning.

- [ ] ... have developed my own model of planning.

- [ ] ... understand the kind of training I will need if I am to pursue the occupations that seem most rewarding to me.

- [ ] ... have made some tentative educational goals to help me stay focused on the kind of career I want to have.

- [ ] ... know more about the realities of the world of work.

- [ ] ... can recognize how people move through the stages of career development.

- [ ] ... know which interpersonal skills work best for me in work situations.

- [ ] ... appreciate that I must be a life-long learner to be successful in life.

- [ ] ... have identified the benchmarks by which I will measure my progress and success in the career-planning process.

- [ ] ... know how my communication skills can affect how others perceive me.

- [ ] ... appreciate how my credibility as a person and as a worker is influenced by my work habits.

- [ ] ... know which friends and family members will be my greatest supporters as I pursue my career goals.

- [ ] ... understand how all of this information comes together to help me plan my career.

A PARENT'S GUIDE TO CAREER DECISION-MAKING

Dear Parent or Guardian:

When your children leave school, they will be entering an increasingly complex world full of challenges. Therefore, we must help them find direction as they begin the process of career building. Children start thinking about careers early, when they dream about "what I want to be when I grow up." They usually associate their dream with a job or occupation. We must teach them that their goal is not a specific job but a career that will reflect their changing life roles--parent, spouse, employee. And, in middle school, we must also give them the life skills they need to adapt to a rapidly changing environment.

The career development program we have adopted asks your children to explore three major questions: Who Am I?; Where Am I Going?; and How Do I Get There? These questions will help them gain self-knowledge and explore the opportunities and challenges the global economy offers. Students will learn the importance of a long-range planning and will develop the skills to nurture their entry into and success in a challenging job. You have a tremendous influence on your child's career decisions. Therefore, we want to involve you and ask you to encourage and support your child as he or she goes through the program.

Occasionally we will ask you to be involved in homework assignments that offer you an opportunity to share your ideas, opinions, stories, and concerns about the career decision-making with your children. We ask you to be open and honest so that they can learn from your experiences.

We are providing this Parent's Guide so that you can understand the kinds of messages we are trying to convey to your children as they begin their career journey. Ask them about the career activities and what they are learning. We hope you enjoy your involvement in the program. Please contact us if you have any questions.

CAREER AS LIFE

Twenty-first century students must consider life and career as synonymous. Their goal is not to "find a job" but to balance five interconnecting life roles:

WORK—finding occupations that provide satisfaction and enough income to meet our responsibilities. Sometimes the role of student is included in this category. However some consider "student" a separate life role, since we must continue learning throughout our lives to keep up with the changing world.

FAMILY—the choices we make to have a meaningful family life. These include choosing life partners, determining the size of our family, nurturing special relationships, and celebrating important occasions.

CITIZEN—the way we contribute to our communities. Some people actively participate in politics and government; some contribute to causes they feel important; still others limit their role to voting and paying taxes.

SPIRITUAL—seeking moral, aesthetic, and/or religious experiences that help to "feed our soul." Most people devote a part of their life/career to improving themselves and their world; a few will make this their life's work.

LEISURE—the way we choose to spend our time when we have a few moments of our own. Leisure must be a significant life role because it helps us balance our other roles and is important to our physical and mental health.

Only by devoting considerable amounts of energy, commitment, and attention to each of these five roles will our children lead successful lives.

STAGES OF CAREER DEVELOPMENT

Career development includes all of a person's life experiences and as such, it evolves as we go through three stages:

Awareness—Beginning at birth and continuing until our death, we must remain open to expanding our perceptions about the world of work and furthering the ongoing process of self-discovery.

Career Exploration—During this stage we investigate and experience. We narrow our career choices to a few feasible alternatives that seem to offer the most satisfaction. We also seek the balance that makes life rewarding. Ultimately, exploration leads to making career decisions.

Career Preparation—Once we make career decisions (and we will make many career decisions during our lives, not just one), we begin planning a realistic path for achieving our career goals. Sometimes the preparation involves education or technical training; other times it may be a matter of laying out a detailed procedure for meeting all the requirements to get to where we want to go.

THE IMPORTANCE OF DECISION-MAKING

Decision-making is one of the most difficult aspects of the career development process. Some people fear making wrong decisions and so avoid making any decisions at all. Some people make quick decisions, which they later regret. Others can't really explain how they make decisions.

We are always making decisions: what we will eat, what route we will take to work, where we will go on vacation, etc. Most of these require little thought or effort. However, occasionally we have to make some very difficult decisions, and good decision-making skills can empower us to make good choices and take appropriate actions.

Many middle-school students face difficult decisions for the first time in their lives. As they begin to assert their independence, they need the decision-making skills that will give them confidence in making their life choices.

Good decision-making involves the following factors:

- Identifying the decision to be made as specifically as possible
- Identifying creative options for the decision
- Exploring the consequences of each choice
- Identifying the personal values associated with the decision
- Setting priorities
- Placing the decisions within the framework of other life goals
- Seeking support and feedback for the different options
- Making the decision
- Determining how to evaluate the quality of the decision

PARENTS CAN ENCOURAGE AND ASSIST THEIR CHILDREN IN ALL PHASES OF DECISION-MAKING

Becoming Involved in Your Child's Career Decisions

Parents play a key role in their child's career and life choices. Working with schools, they can create a learning environment that empowers their children to make those critical choices. Here are some significant roles you can play in your child's career development:

- **Reflective Learner:** Share what you have learned from your own career. What was most rewarding? What would you do differently? Explain how even bad experiences have helped you to learn and grow. Explain how examining your values, priorities, and needs helped you in your career decision-making.

- **Role Model:** Children are keen observers of their parents. They watch how we approach work tasks, observe our levels of commitment to our work, and note the skills we use to do our job effectively. They also notice our negative reactions to work and the effects of work on our attitudes and behavior. Discuss the positive and negative aspects of your work with your child and explain how you handle them.

- **Information Source:** Children need information about the workplace and about the resources available to help them make career decisions. Help them network and learn about the tools that can assist them in finding the up-to-date information they need.

- **Listener:** The dictionary defines listen as to hear with thoughtful attention. Listen to the dreams, the concerns, the hopes, the uncertainties, and the excitement of your children. Listen to how they are making career decisions. Listen to their requests for help. Really listen.

- **Instructor:** Teach your children the life skills they will need: communication skills, problem-solving skills, time management skills, negotiation skills, social skills, organizational skills, etc. Discuss how you learned and applied these skills.

- **Opportunity Maker:** Exploration is a powerful tool in narrowing choices and making decisions. Help your children observe people at work, use electronic resources, or participate in experiential learning to explore the work world.

- **Stabilizer:** Help your children balance the five interrelated life roles: worker, family member, citizen, individual at leisure, and spiritual being. Setting limits is one step in creating the needed balance.

- **Motivator:** Your interest in your children's career journey is their best motivator. Having high but realistic aspirations helps them strive for excellence. Encourage their participation in school-based career activities and point out their relevance to the world of work so that they maintain a focus on learning. Help them discover their talents.

DEVELOPMENTAL ISSUES

The middle school years can be a troubling time for parents and children alike. As they approach adolescence, children move from dependence on adults and take on more responsibility for their lives. It is a time for adjustments. As both parents and adolescents try out new behaviors, they create a different kind of environment that accommodates the changes.

Some major developmental issues with which early adolescents typically contend are the following:

• Developing an identity—looking for an integrated sense of who they are

• Testing roles in social and work situations

• Seeking independence—without losing the security of past relationships

• Risk-taking and experimentation

• Looking for approval—often from anyone who will give it

• Developing a sense of competence

• Integrating the factors related to self-esteem

• Searching for comfort levels for daily routines and relationships

• Developing skills and attitudes that provide a sense of individual power

• Achieving more mature social relationships

• Developing attitudes toward social groups and institutions

• Accepting strengths and limitations

If you are aware of these issues you can recognize some of the reasons young adolescents seem to be struggling with their existence. Your children should be struggling a bit because the challenges facing them are significant. However, your love, support, reasonable boundaries, and common sense can provide the foundation for them to flourish in this time of tremendous change.